THE
40-DAY

SURRENDER
FAST
FOR TEENS

DR. CELESTE OWENS
WITH
AALIYAH OWENS

good success
PUBLISHING

Good Success Publishing

The 40-Day Surrender Fast for Teens
Copyright © 2020 by Celeste Owens

This book is also available as an ebook. Visit www.surrendershop.com

Requests for information should be addressed to:
Good Success Publishing, P.O. Box 5072, Upper Marlboro, MD 20775

ISBN: 9781735588209 (softcover)

Library of Congress Control Number:

This book is printed on acid-free paper.

All scripture quotations, unless otherwise indicated, are taken from the Contemporary English Version. Copyright © 1995 by American Bible Society. Used by permission. All rights reserved.

Cover design: Alexey Zgola
Interior design: Alexey Zgola

Printed in the United States of America

When I did the Surrender Fast I surrendered social media. This taught me that there is actually so much more stuff you can occupy your time with. You have to balance your schedule so you can do other things that interest you. Maybe even give social media a break for a while. It was also easier to better myself without social media, and now I don't even use it that much. Unless I'm doing something and it's required.

Vaniah Carter
Age 14

I have surrendered a lot of things, but one of my greatest Surrender was when I was 17 years old, I surrendered secular music. I was really into secular music for most of my teen years .When I gave my life to Christ, I was really convinced that secular music was never God's will. I surrendered secular music in 2019. Am happy to testify to the world on what the Lord has done in me. Secular music is now total noise in my ears. I can't withstand it at all. God is also using me greatly in His work now. I believe that His purpose in my life will be established because of the surrendered path I took. I give God the Glory.

Moureen Ayuma Owens Munyasa
Kenya, Mombasa
Age 19

I had an amazing experience with the 40 day Surrender Fast for Teens! The experience with Dr. Celeste taught me new things about the Bible that I did not know before. It was a challenge for me at first getting to know the others on the fast, but then it got easier. The best thing about the fast was learning more about Christ and how to apply biblical principles to my life. In conclusion, I really loved the Surrender Fast and Dr. Celeste for teaching me how to live a better life.

Isaiah Richards
Age 14

I completed *The 40-Day Surrender Fast for Kids* in 2016. I fasted from my favorite TV show, My Little Pony! I fasted specifically for my asthma. After I finished the fast, I didn't have an asthma attack for the next year!

Joy Barnett
Age 15

Dedicated to every teen
that surrenders,
no matter the cost.

CONTENTS

ACKNOWLEDGEMENTS FROM AALIYAH

To God: Thank you for allowing me to be on the most awesome journey with You. I know the best is yet to come.

To Dad and Mom: Y'all have always been there for me even when I don't want your attention. Thanks for being loyal parents.

To AJ: I honestly just really enjoy your company. IDK how children go through life without a sibling. Thanks for being there!

To Ms. KC: Although we don't see each other all the time, you have helped me go places like Kenya and reach my goals. You are one of the nicest people I know.

To TJ: Thank you for helping us with the book cover design. You are so creative.

To Maureen: Thank you for being my sister from Kenya. You are beautiful and a big help getting the word about surrender around Kenya.

To Ms. Cherise and Ms. Janelle: Thank you for leading the teens in fasting. You don't know what impact you have had.

INTRODUCTION

I n 2010, my mom created *The 40-Day Surrender Fast* book. At the time I was really young, so I didn't really understand the importance of the book. When I did the Surrender Fast the first time at age 8, I surrendered candy. That wasn't something that kept me from God, but it was something that I liked very much. So it was a sacrifice.

I was fasting because I wanted God to make this girl in my class stop bullying everyone. After I fasted, she was still a bully, but she didn't bully as much and I was no longer afraid of her. That made me feel powerful. The next year she left our school.

Now it is your turn. What will you surrender to God? Make sure it is something that is a sacrifice. The goal is to get closer to God, but it is also okay to fast and ask God to do something in your life. But even if He doesn't answer your prayer the way you want, remember again the most important part of your fast is to get closer to Him.

Each chapter of the Surrender Fast are the words that my mom wrote to her friends in 2010. She hasn't changed the words for you. We believe you will be able to understand and follow it easily. Now you get to follow along like you are doing the Surrender Fast them. It's fun! And challenging, so get ready.

You're probably wondering how much time will this take everyday?!

All you have to do is commit 15 minutes of your time. You will be happy that you did.

So here we go. Welcome to the Surrender Fast! My mom and I pray that your life will never be the same.

THIS IS HOW TO DO THE SURRENDER FAST:

It's me, Dr. Celeste. My daughter, Aaliyah, tells me that teens don't read Introductions. Please prove her wrong and read this very important section :)

1. **Seek God for guidance**. Pray and ask God what He would have you surrender for the next 40 days. By way of example, some teens have fasted from junk food, fear, television, social media, secular music, and/or jealousy.

2. **Read the Pre-Fast Preparation section**. Ideally, these chapters should be read one per day for at least 5 days prior to the start of your fast. However, they could be read two per day or all in one sitting. No matter your method of choice, be sure to meditate

on each passage and journal what you sense God is saying to you.

3. **Begin the 40-Day Surrender Fast.** Start each day with prayer, and this devotional. There is a chapter for each weekday (Monday - Friday). All you need to do is make a 15-minute commitment each day. Complete your reading and the Personal Time with God #PTWG section.

4. **Ask a friend to fast with you**. It helps to have another teen or adult available for accountability and encouragement. Most people who have done the Surrender Fast have done so with at least one other person.

5. **Enjoy the journey**. Don't be too hard on yourself during the 40 days. A closer walk with God, not perfection is the goal. Therefore, seek Him with all your heart, surrender your will for His, and watch Him do some amazing things in your life.

Let God Do a New Thing!

You may be wondering, "Why am I fasting?" It's not you, it's God. He is bringing you closer to Him and in the next few days, He will call you to do something you hadn't considered and change the whole course of your life.

As some of you know, I have been home all year. At the close of 2009, God called me to leave all that I knew—private practice, speaking, writing, ministry duties—to go to a place He would disclose. I soon discovered that the undisclosed location was my house!

So at the top of 2010, I found myself home with two little ones and plenty of time to be with God. I must admit I questioned God's plan at first, but as I look back over the last nine months I am thankful that He redirected the course of my life and changed me in ways quite unexpected. Now He wants to do the same for you.

God is calling you to do something different—to move out of your comfort zone. Don't resist and don't let fear keep you from what He has in store. Isaiah 43:18-19 reads:

Forget what happened long ago!
Don't think about the past.
I am creating something new.
There it is! Do you see it?
I have put roads in deserts,
streams in thirsty lands.

Yes, God can and will do all that for you.

What is the secret desire of your heart? He knows, but won't move without your full cooperation and a complete surrender of your will. And that's where this fast comes in. In the next week, because you are seeking change, you are going to surrender some habit or belief to God for 40 days. We will start the journey together this Monday.

I have done two 40-Day Fasts since April. Each time with other people (i.e., corporate fasting) and we have been miraculously changed. This time, God has called me to do it with you via blog. I will explain more tomorrow.

Les Brown says, "If you want to make this your decade, you've got to decide to be bold, to take life on." Don't leave the year the same way you came in. The former things have passed; God wants to do a new thing in you.

PERSONAL TIME WITH GOD
#PTWG

AALIYAH'S AFFIRMATION CORNER: I won't leave this year the same way I came in. All the old stuff I'm going to leave in the pass. God wants to do a new thing in my life.

WHAT'S THIS VERSE ABOUT?
Isaiah 43:18-19

_____

_____

_____

KEEPING IT REAL: Do you think there are some things you should stop? What are they? Will you let go?

_____

_____

_____

PRAYER CORNER: Dear Heavenly Father, I thank you because I am showing up to say yes to your will. Do a new thing for me and in me. Show up in an amazing way today; demonstrate your power and your willingness to do something out of the ordinary for me. My dependence is on you God. Move as only you can move. I ask these things in the matchless name of Jesus. Amen.

What is a Surrender Fast?

According to the Merriam-Webster Dictionary, to surrender is to give oneself up into the power of another, especially as a prisoner. Likewise, when one is arrested what's the first thing that he does? He raises his hands in an act of surrender and submits to the authority of a higher power. That type of surrender—releasing your will and plan in favor of God's—is what this fast is all about.

I am near completion of a book that I believe will change the way this generation approaches success. It outlines the steps that every person must take to fulfill his/her destiny. The fifth step on this journey is "Isolation" and the proper conclusion to this stage is a fast. Jesus modeled this for us. During His time of isolation in the wilderness, He fasted for 40 days and nights from food and drink (Matthew 4:1-11). As a reward for His complete surrender to God's plan, He was ushered into His destiny. I formulated this fast, and subsequently named it *The 40-Day Surrender Fast*, based on Jesus' time of fasting in the wilderness.

My first experience with the Surrender Fast was in April of 2010. While attending a women's fellowship at the First

Baptist Church of Glenarden, Pastor John K. Jenkins Sr. taught on the disciplines of a godly woman. I was instantly convicted about my lack of discipline in the area of diet. For many years, God had been dealing with me about my eating habits. Even as a three-year survivor of breast cancer, I was content to eat what I liked, despite my knowledge of the link between diet and disease. I was so controlled by food that I was willing to hinder my physical and spiritual health for the momentary thrill of a box of Hot Tamales! I knew that God was displeased and I was desperate for a change.

So on that Saturday morning in April I cried. And when my crying had ended, I decided to do what God had been instructing me to do for years. I surrendered my will for His in this area.

I chose to do the Daniel Fast. During my time of fasting, I shared my testimony with other women and a few of them joined me. Each of us fasted from something different, one from TV, another sugar, but our hearts were in concert together as we collectively surrendered our wills. Initially, the fast was difficult for me, but somewhere around day 31, and much to my surprise, I decided to become a vegetarian and I haven't looked back since.

So now it's your turn. If you are feeling stuck, frustrated, and/or bound, decide that now is the time to do something new; have the courage to release your plan for His. The blessings that will stem from your obedience will be well worth the sacrifice (see Deuteronomy 28).

#PTWG

AALIYAH'S AFFIRMATION CORNER: I will no longer be stuck, frustrated, or held back. I am going to let God do something new in me. It might not be easy, but it will be worth it.

WHAT'S THIS VERSE ABOUT?
Deuteronomy 28:1

_____

_____

_____

KEEPING IT REAL: Have you ever fasted? If yes, did you learn anything from it?

_____

_____

_____

PRAYER CORNER: Dear Heavenly Father I surrender all to you; my plans, my will, and my life. Whatever I specifically need to surrender to you, make it abundantly clear and then give me the courage to release. It won't be easy, but it will be worth it. I seal this prayer in the mighty name of Jesus. Amen.

Bold and Courageous

Celeste, just as I instructed Joshua, 'Be bold and courageous' is what God has been urging all year. In an effort to make this command MY TRUTH, I have read and re-read the book of Joshua. It has changed me tremendously, but there is still more that God wants to do. That's the reason He has called me to this fast (and dragged you in with me); I need to be released. I can no longer allow the hurts of the past to dictate my actions and keep me from being bold and courageous. He needs me to be an ambassador of His word and if I am timid and shy I won't be an effective witness.

My lack of boldness came to a head the other day. I was helping a candidate solicit votes at a polling site. While there, I ran into a colleague who was campaigning for a different candidate. After a few pleasantries, we got into a conversation about the other candidates that were running for office that term. She disagreed, quite vehemently, with my choices and sought to change my mind.

Suffice it to say, it worked. By the time she was done, I had changed one of my votes. To make matters worse, I looked for her after I voted to let her know that I had been persuaded by her argument. Fortunately, I couldn't get her approval; she had left the site. I realized immediately that that interaction had been a set up. God had my attention.

I relay this embarrassing story to highlight my need for God—especially in this area. Last night I prayed for insight into my behavior. God revealed to me that I lose myself when I am around aggressive/assertive people; I don't feel empowered to appropriately handle their type.

The root of the problem dates back to grade school. I desperately wanted to fit in, but didn't. I was continuously rejected by (at least in my mind) the aggressive, sometimes mean, yet overwhelmingly popular "it" girls.

At the same time, I was overly invested in pleasing my authority figures believing, in error, that their approval would make me good and acceptable. All lies. God's acceptance of me is all that matters.

I am learning day by day that He loves me just the way I am. As I grow closer to Him, I gain the courage to be just who I am. Before this year is out, I will be firm in my identity, sure of my calling, and ready for any and every assignment that comes my way. Because of Christ and the work that He did for me on the cross, I am whole and complete in God.

I read this morning, "Don't be afraid or ashamed and don't be discouraged. You won't be disappointed. Forget how sinful you were when you were young" (Isaiah 54:4a). He was reminding me that I am not that scared little girl who had no voice and needed acceptance. I am a bold and courageous woman in Christ. I am also reminded that God will give us double for our trouble (see Isaiah 61:7) and make up for all of the hurts we have experienced.

We will boldly declare, this day, that we are healed from the pains and wounds of the past; we are new in Christ, and equipped to succeed in all that we put our hands to. So for the next 40 days, starting Monday, September 13, I am fasting from a timid and fearful attitude, especially as it relates to aggressive/assertive people. I will speak as the Spirit leads and I will not let fear shut me down. What will you surrender to God?

#PTWG

————○○○○———— ⬤ ————○○○○————

AALIYAH'S AFFIRMATION CORNER: I am healed from the pains and wounds of the past; I am new in Christ, and everything I put my hands to succeeds!

WHAT'S THIS VERSE ABOUT?
Isaiah 61:7

_____

_____

_____

KEEPING IT REAL: What are some weaknesses you choose not to open up about? Write it below. Next, share this with the friend that's fasting with you, or a parent or sibling.

_____

_____

_____

PRAYER CORNER: Father, I am not where we want to be, but thank you that I am not where I used to be. Each day I am getting stronger, wiser, and better equipped to take on the challenges before me. I declare and decree that I am whole in you and that no weapon formed against me will prosper. Lastly, thank you for Father for never giving up on me. Your plan for me is still good and I thank you for that. I seal this prayer by faith. Amen.

Why 40 Days?

The number 40 is significant for several reasons. One, it is universally accepted as a number of importance to God not only for the frequency of its occurrence in the Bible but also for its association with a period of trial and probation. For example:

▶ In Noah's day the rains fell for 40 days and nights (Genesis 7:4)

▶ The children of Israel wandered in the wilderness for 40 years (Joshua 5:6)

▶ Goliath presented himself to Israel for 40 days (1 Samuel 17:16)

▶ David reigned over Israel for 40 years (2 Samuel 5:4; 1 Kings 2:11)

▶ Jesus fasted 40 days and 40 nights (Matthew 4:2)

▶ Jesus was tempted 40 days (Luke 4:2; Mark 1:13)

And just as an aside, women are pregnant for 40 weeks.

Secondly, the number 40 is significant because it appears to be, at least from my experiences, the right amount of time needed to break a stronghold. You may have read, and research indicates that it takes about 21 days to make or break a habit. This may be true, but a stronghold is something different; it's a habit gone wild. In the spiritual, a stronghold is an incorrect pattern of thinking that influences how we live our lives. For that reason, 40 days appears to be the more accurate number for breaking a stronghold.

Strongholds can be evident in many areas of our lives, but one area where they can be especially detrimental is in our emotional life. After years of hurt, we naturally seek to protect our emotions. In a futile attempt to ward off further pain, we often adopt incorrect beliefs (e.g., people will always hurt me so I shouldn't let anyone get too close). These erroneous beliefs don't allow us to move as God instructs and keep us from taking the risks that are necessary for success.

In and of ourselves we are hopeless to change, but with God, all things are possible. His healing virtue tears down the walls that have kept us confined and His grace propels us further than we ever thought we could go.

This is my third time doing this particular 40-day fast (the first time I fasted from certain types of foods and the second from pride and selfishness). Each time I noticed a distinct pattern. The first 21 days were challenging, I couldn't see how God was going to change me. Right around day 21, I started sensing that change was on the way. About day 30, I started noticing consistent changes in my behavior. And by day 40, I was healed; a new me was restored and renewed in spirit, soul and body.

The scripture reminds us that some things only change through prayer and fasting (see Mark 9:29). Are you ready to be free and released from your stronghold? If so, this is your time of probation; your chance to prove to God and yourself that you are ready to accept the new thing that He has for you. Commit yourself to this fast and see God do a mighty work in your life.

#PTWG

AALIYAH'S AFFIRMATION CORNER: I can't change myself, but with God all things are possible. He is healing me and tearing down the walls that have kept me from being my true self. I am going to show up in the world because the world needs me.

WHAT'S THIS VERSE ABOUT?
Mark 9:29

_____

_____

_____

KEEPING IT REAL: What are some things in your life that are keeping you away from God? Are you willing to surrender one of them for 40 days?

_____

_____

_____

PRAYER CORNER: Father, I am nothing without you. Please saturate me with your presence today. I want to be one with you. Whatever things I have latched onto or whatever things have attached themselves to me, I pray that you set me free during my time of prayer and fasting. Touch me as only you can. Illuminate my path as I make my way back home to you. And with open arms you will receive me, because you are just that kind of God; gracious, merciful and full of compassion. Thank you for receiving this prayer. In Jesus' name I pray. Amen.

Who Am I?

Within the "Info" section of a Facebook page, participants are invited to respond to the prompt "relationship status." The normal responses are single, married, divorced, etc. However, once in a while someone responds: *it's complicated*. That leads me to believe that they are in a relationship but not *really* in a relationship—that is complicated.

The same can be true when it comes to healing from childhood emotional wounds: it's complicated. The mere passing of time doesn't make us whole. Simply saying the words "I'm over that" doesn't make it so, nor does burying the pain deep in the recesses of our mind. Healing is a process and if most of us are honest, we know that getting over our past is—well—complicated.

As a child I was sensitive; every harsh word and disapproving look wounded me. Because of my sensitive nature, I quickly adopted the belief that I wasn't good enough. That false belief, which shaped my worldview for many years, became the foundation for my identity and produced fruit. This is how that belief influenced my thought life and behavior:

The false belief:

I AM NOT GOOD ENOUGH

The fruit of that belief:

1. A poor self-mage that led to the following beliefs:
    a. If my peers accept me (especially the popular ones) that makes me good.
    b. If I associate with those who *others* perceive as good I, by association, will be good too.
    c. If I am pleasing to those who are in authority, they will like me and infer goodness upon me.
2. A propensity for perfectionism:
    a. If I become perfect in every way (i.e., style of dress, talk, education, hair, makeup, etc.), no one will ever learn my secret shame—that I am not good enough.

If you can't follow that it's okay because *it's complicated*; lies always are.

There are some of you who are fighting with God. He is telling you to fast from a certain belief or behavior that you believe you are "over" and you are refusing to re-visit that old issue. Well, if God is leading you to do so, He knows that there is some rotten fruit that still needs picking.

Today, I know I am good enough but the fruit of pleasing (especially authority) still lingers (see blog post *Bold and Courageous*). But I declare at the end of these

40 days that fruit will be no more. God finds me pleasing and that is all that matters.

The scripture tells us that we must bring every thought into captivity to the obedience of Christ (see 2 Corinthians 10:5). The only way to challenge every rebellious thought is to study and meditate on God's word; let His truth become your truth.

Here's His truth. You don't need anyone to approve of or accept you because God loves you just the way you are (see I John 4:19). If you meditate on His word day and night, do all that it says, you will make your way prosperous and have good success (see Joshua 1:8).

Now that's the truth and the truth is never complicated.

#PTWG

AALIYAH'S AFFIRMATION CORNER: I don't need anyone to approve of or accept me because God loves me just the way I am. If I meditate on His word day and night, do all that it says, I will make my way prosperous and I will have good success.

WHAT'S THIS VERSE ABOUT?
2 Corinthians 10:5

_____

_____

_____

KEEPING IT REAL: What lies have people told you that you have accepted as truth? Are they really true about you? Why or why not?

_____

_____

_____

PRAYER CORNER: Dear God, as I end the Pre-Fast Preparation period, help me to feel your presence and your love. Give me the courage to dig deep and uproot any untruth and replace that lie with YOUR truth. YOU LOVE ME AND YOU APPROVE OF ME! In Jesus' name I pray. Amen.

Expect the Unexpected

The Lord says:
"My thoughts and my ways are not like yours.
Just as the heavens are higher than the earth,
my thoughts and my ways are higher than yours.
(Isaiah 55:8-9)

Welcome to Day 1 of the Surrender Fast! If your life is anything like mine, God has already started working on your heart and making it ready to receive more of Him.

We are a diverse group: men and women, young and seasoned, from the USA to other countries around the world. What we're surrendering is also quite varied. Some are fasting from food, some from lack of trust; while others relinquish fear, selfishness, pride, and insecurity. Each journey will be different, but we are all united in a single cause: to draw closer to God. I encourage you to keep notes and journal your experience.

As you have learned from reading the Pre-Fast Preparation posts, I am surrendering timidity to God. I will no longer be fearful but bold and courageous. For the next 40 days, I will actively listen to the Holy Spirit's direction and step out boldly as He leads.

So God's first assignment...read about humility. That wasn't quite the direction I was expecting but I know from my other two fasts to expect the unexpected. The scripture tells us that God's ways are not our ways, nor His thoughts our thoughts.

So in obedience I am reading "Humility" by Andrew Murray. He says that humility is the place of total dependence on God. He further writes:

Humility is not a thing we bring to God. It is also not a thing God gives to us. It is simply the realization of what nothings we really are, when we truly see how God is Everything, and when we clear out room in our hearts so that He can be everything for us.

I certainly want God to be my everything. Therefore, each morning I will commit my time to God: I will pray, read His word, and meditate on what I have read. You must make the same commitment. Growth won't occur by osmosis; a dream comes with much business and painful effort (see Ecclesiastes 5:3). If you want to experience a new thing in God, you must do your part. Hence, humble yourself before the King of Glory, listen to His instructions, and move as He directs. Freedom is on the way.

#PTWG

AALIYAH'S AFFIRMATION CORNER: Dreams come true when I believe in them and do the work. If I want to be great in this world, I must do my part.

WHAT'S THIS VERSE ABOUT?
Isaiah 55:8-9

_____
_____
_____

KEEPING IT REAL: What does it mean to be humble? Do you think being humble makes you look weak? What is the difference between being a pushover and being humble?

_____
_____
_____

PRAYER CORNER: Father, beginnings are always exciting, but it's the middle and end that can be challenging. So empower me to commit and finish the Surrender Fast. Please show up everyday and let me know that you are near. Thank you for being a good Father. In Jesus' name I pray. Amen.

Time, Effort, Reward

> Plow your fields,
> scatter seeds of justice,
> and harvest faithfulness.
> Worship me, the Lord,
> and I will send my saving power
> down like rain.
>
> *(Hosea 10:12)*

I t is said that time plus effort equals reward. This philosophy is true for most of everything in life, present fast included. God has promised you a "new thing" and that promise most likely prompted you to join this fast. Therefore, be assured that He sees your sacrifice and will reward you according to your investment. In other words, over the next 38 days the time that you spend investing in your relationship with God will pay off handsomely.

The scripture tells us that you will harvest what you plant (see Galatians 6:7). We are also reminded that a few seeds make a small harvest, but a lot of seeds make a big harvest (see II Corinthians 9:6). Like you, I am expecting a mighty move of God during the course of this fast so I am sowing generously, but sowing requires a sacrifice. Therefore, I am making my comfort of little importance. I am neglecting that extra hour of sleep and cutting out activities that hinder my ability to seek God with all my heart. What about you? Are you investing in what matters? I know it's only day 2 but a strong finish requires a strong start.

For that reason, surrender your maladaptive habits to the Lord. Allow Him to break up the fallow, unfruitful ground in your heart and seed it with His plans and purposes. Seek Him with all that is in you, and require His favor until He comes and rains righteousness upon you.

The new thing you seek is here but your possession of it requires time and effort. Thus, rise early in the morning to give Him praise and seek His direction through prayer and the reading of His word. This little investment of your time will reap an abundant reward.

#PTWG

AALIYAH'S AFFIRMATION CORNER: When I work hard, it pays off. I am going to give my best effort to everything I do because I am worth it!

WHAT'S THIS VERSE ABOUT?
Hosea 10:12

KEEPING IT REAL: You must work hard at your goals. Do you finish what you start? Or do you quit when things get hard?

PRAYER CORNER: God I'm not praying for victory today because I am already victorious. Please just help me make it to the finish line. I am a winner, I am chosen by You. You will see me through. Amen.

Rebuild and Renew

Then they will rebuild cities
that have been in ruins
for many generations.

(Isaiah 61:4)

Yesterday's blog revealed a basic truth: an investment of time and effort reaps a reward. What a marvelous reason to rejoice. Surrendering certainly has its benefits. In another 37 days we will have the benefit of a more intimate relationship with God, improved emotional health, and breakthroughs in many other areas of our lives.

Yet God has revealed another benefit. Let me invite you to think outside the box; beyond your short-sided view of reality. This fast has benefits that extend way beyond you. Ephesians 3:20 reads, "I pray that Christ Jesus and the church will forever bring praise to God. His power at work in us can do far more than we dare to ask or imagine. Amen."

How many of you have been praying for your families and praying for God's favor and the miracle that only He can perform? The time is now; the shift is occurring. You can't see it in the natural but in the spiritual change is here.

That brother you have been praying for, God is doing in Him what He has promised. That child who has strayed, God is bringing her back. Those generational curses— debt, depression, molestation, anger, broken marriages, abandonment—God is making new.

Your radical act of faith is doing the impossible. Your surrender delights God. The scripture reminds us to, "Do what the Lord wants, and He will give you your heart's desire" (Psalm 37:4).

God is now excited about acting on your behalf. Because of YOU He is repairing the ancient cities and the devastation of many generations; he is restoring the breaches. What a marvelous thing He is doing. Rejoice for it because it is already done!

Think about it. What abundant thing will God do for you and your family as a result of this fast? What generational curses will He break? I am the oldest of eight. Seven of us have accepted Christ as our personal savior. I declare, in Jesus' name that He will save my brother Stephen within the 38 days that we have left. We (me and my three sisters who are also on this fast) are rejoicing for it is already done.

#PTWG

AALIYAH'S AFFIRMATION CORNER: My radical act of faith is doing the impossible. My surrender delights God.

WHAT'S THIS VERSE ABOUT?
Isaiah 61:4

_____

_____

_____

KEEPING IT REAL: Families follow patterns. Like in some families there is a lot of divorce or poverty. What generational curses are you asking God to break in your family? Do you believe that He can do it?

_____

_____

_____

PRAYER CORNER: Lord I thank you for this day. I thank you for the opportunity to come face-to-face with some things that have troubled me about my families for some time. Lord, give me the grace to be a change agent; give me the courage to declare that some familial patterns will be broken because of this time of fasting. I ask these things in the mighty name of Jesus. Amen.

The Other Side

That evening, Jesus said to his disciples,
"Let's cross to the east side."

(Mark 4:35)

'll let you in on a little secret…blogging is not my comfort zone, neither is writing for that matter. I do them both in obedience to God. That first Monday I blogged, I was amazed at what God wrote through me and excited for what He was to do for His people. However, the overwhelming response to the post sent me into a near panic as I thought, *"I can't do that again; I can't deliver another piece that will speak to the hearts of so many."* But as I let the Holy Spirit speak to my emotional storm, His peace enveloped me and calmed my fears.

The disciples experienced a similar panic in Mark, Chapter 4. One evening, after a long day of ministering, Jesus announced that they would cross to the other side. No doubt this was an exciting moment. *What new adventures would they experience on the other side?* Well, no sooner had they begun their journey, they experienced a storm.

Needless to say, the disciples hadn't anticipated such an occurrence. This storm was of monstrous proportion and they panicked. But what they did next is what we all are to do in the midst of a storm—they cried out to Jesus. In an instant, He made the winds and sea behave and brought an immediate calm.

Likewise, Jesus has said to each of you, "Let's cross to the other side." In other words, "Let me do a new thing." No doubt your excitement is great: *what might this other side bring?* Don't be surprised when it's a storm.

Each morning before each post and in the midst of my emotional storm, I remind myself that I am doing His work not mine. Armed with that truth, I take a deep breath, whisper a prayer, read my word, and write. The peace that envelops me during this process calms my fear and allows me to have an experience with God like no other.

Let His peace rest on you as well. For the next 36 days, remember that you are not making these sacrifices in your own strength. Whatever He has asked you to release to Him, is His will and you will succeed. "What God has planned for people who love him is more than eyes have seen or ears have heard. It has never even entered our minds!" (I Corinthians 2:9). Be blessed.

#PTWG

AALIYAH'S AFFIRMATION CORNER: Whatever He has asked me to release to Him is His will and I will succeed because I am obedient.

WHAT'S THIS VERSE ABOUT?
Mark 4:35

_____

_____

_____

KEEPING IT REAL: What storms or bad circumstances have started in your life as a result of your fast? Are you going to give up or push through?

_____

_____

_____

PRAYER CORNER: Thank you God for the reminder that you are with me in the midst of the storm. Thank you for keeping me and protecting me from dangers seen and unseen. It is by your might that I move, breath, and have my being. Not just in the good times, but also in the bad. So I will keep my mind on you so that I can have perfect peace, even in the midst of the storm. I seal this prayer by faith. Amen.

It Will Come to Pass

Everything God says is true—
and it's a shield for all
who come to him for safety.

(Proverbs 30:5)

It may not look like it right now, but every promise that God has made to you will come to pass. If you abide in Him, He will protect you and the dream He planted in your heart so long ago.

It's easy to become discouraged and discontent from today's vantage point. But our "now" doesn't necessarily reflect our tomorrow. The scripture reads, "we are already God's children, though what we will be hasn't yet been seen" (I John 3:2a). I don't know about you, but in a year's time, I won't be what I am today. Better yet, in 35 days, I won't be what I am today. Each day I am improving and growing in Him.

Over the years, many of godly words have been spoken over me. It has been said that I will have the "ministry of marriage" and that I will be speaking to thousands. None of that is evident right now. Andel and I have a great marriage, but we aren't ministering to couples. I speak publicly, but certainly not to thousands.

Does that mean those things aren't coming to pass? Absolutely not!

It is written, if you are faithful over a few He will make you ruler over many (see Matthew 25:23). Likewise, the word encourages us to appreciate the day of small beginnings, for it is in this time of preparation that He makes us ready for the greater things of Him (see Zechariah 4:10).

Therefore, I am using each day to prepare for what is to come. Andel and I regularly fast for the welfare of couples, and I speak with zeal to every audience that comes under the sound of my voice. In God's timing, I will transcend to greater heights in Him; but it's what I do today—in excellence—that builds the firm foundation for what is to come.

Beloved, don't let today stifle your hopes for tomorrow. Keep the faith; God's word will not return to Him void. He promises that not one of all the good things He has spoken concerning you will fail and ALL will come to pass (see Joshua 21:45, 23:14).

#PTWG

---○---

AALIYAH'S AFFIRMATION CORNER: God's word will not return to Him unanswered. Whatever he promised to me, He will do it for me. I am going to just keep believing.

WHAT'S THIS VERSE ABOUT?
Proverbs 30:5

_____

_____

_____

KEEPING IT REAL: What promises have God spoken to you that have yet to come to pass? Do you believe that He will do it?

_____

_____

_____

PRAYER CORNER: God help me to believe with all my heart that your plans can't be stopped. Let me trust that they will come to pass, no matter what it looks like right now. Show me what preparations I need to make today, to see the manifestation of your glory tomorrow. Open my eyes so that I can see in the spirit and guard my mouth so that I speak life. Thank for answering my prayer. In the name of Jesus I pray. Amen.

DAY 6

#PTWG

Scripture(s):

How is God speaking to you today through His Word, through people, or any other way?

#PTWG

Scripture(s):

How is God speaking to you today through His Word, through people, or any other way?

Establish Your Faith

Ask me, and I will do whatever you ask. This way the Son will bring honor to the Father.

I will do whatever you ask me to do.

(John 14:13-14)

I am excited to report that my first big bold and courageous moment occurred this weekend as I ministered to the Cancer Support Ministry of the First Baptist Church of Glenarden. It was a powerful session.

My parents, in town for a short visit, attended the seminar and shared some words of encouragement to the group. One statement made by my mother struck a chord with me. She said that she would never get cancer. That is a bold statement considering that she has an extensive family history of various cancers and statistics conclude that she too will suffer with the disease. But she knows that God isn't moved by statistics and His plan will come to pass no matter her history. That's why when He had instructed her (at a prior speaking engagement) to declare that she would never get cancer, she did. And she had been saying it ever since.

I had never made such a declaration and didn't intend to do so that day, but as I stood before the people the words

"I will never be stricken with cancer again in Jesus' Name" came out of my mouth. I felt both a mix of excitement and power as I proclaimed what I knew to be true. And in that moment, I established my faith.

Establishing or activating your faith is the process of doing in the natural what God has already finished in the spiritual. The scripture declares that faith without deeds is useless (James 2:20) and that without faith it is impossible to please the Lord (see Hebrews 11:6). Therefore, on that Saturday, I did what God had been urging me to do for months. Let me explain.

Just a few months prior to this even I had spoken at a cancer fundraising event. During the speech, I made the statement "I don't believe that I will get cancer again, but if I do I will trust God for my healing." I felt a little strange making that statement and I didn't understand why, but now I do. We are told in Proverbs 18:21 that words can bring death or life and in James 3:10 that the tongue can speak both blessings and curses. I now know that when I said the words, "I don't believe that I will...but if I do..." my doubt left room for the disease to attack me again.

For that reason, on Saturday, September 18, 2010 in Conference Room 2, before a group of cancer survivors, God challenged me to establish my faith. To say aloud the words my soul had longed to hear, *I will never be stricken with cancer again in Jesus' Name.* Now if that isn't bold and courageous, I don't know what is!

Some of you are wondering: *how can she make such a claim? How can she say with certainty that she will never get cancer again?* I can do so because God's word gives me permission. Jesus said that I can ask anything in His name and He will do it. Furthermore, when I am living a life surrendered unto Him, I am able to accurately discern His will and know what to ask for.

My friends, faith is more than mere words; it is an attitude of confidence that knows without a shadow of doubt that God will do just as He has promised. I implore you today, and for the next 32 days, to establish your faith with boldness and watch His will come to pass. Be blessed in Jesus' Name.

#PTWG

---○○---•---○○---

AALIYAH'S AFFIRMATION CORNER: Faith is more than what you say, it is an attitude that says there is nothing impossible for God and He keeps His promises.

WHAT'S THIS VERSE ABOUT?
John 14:13-14

_____

_____

_____

KEEPING IT REAL: Has God ever spoken a promise to you? If so, what was it and has it happened yet?

_____

_____

_____

PRAYER CORNER: Dear Lord, thank you for being Jehovah Rapha, my healer. I pray healing for myself; may you heal me in a miraculous way. Would you not just heal me in the body, but also in my mind? Lord, if my mind is making me sick, I pray that you cause me to know this truth so that I am made free. Keep me from worry, keep me from reacting negatively to stress, and keep me in perfect peace as I keep my mind on you. And lastly, may you make me whole: spirit, mind, and body. I thank you for this miracle. In Jesus' name I pray. Amen.

Pray for Your Enemies

Don't be happy to see your enemies trip and fall down.
The Lord will find out and be unhappy.
 Then he will stop being angry with them.
(Proverbs 24:17-18)

I f you have lived any amount of time someone has wronged you. Some offenses have been slight while others major. Nonetheless, the Bible gives clear instructions on how to handle these offenses. It states, "But I tell you to love your enemies and pray for anyone who mistreats you," (Matthew 5:44).

It's human nature to wish bad on someone who has hurt you, to seek revenge, and/or shut down emotionally. However, a mature Christian, one that has matured in love, accesses the power surging within him to respond in a way that defies his nature. The scripture reads, "Christ gives me the strength to face anything" (Philippians 4:13). That includes forgiving those who spitefully use you.

It's easy to love those who love you, but the proof of your conversion is reflected in your ability to love those who use you, who take advantage of your kindness, and wish harm upon you.

Christ experienced similar maltreatment. During His public ministry He was rejected, talked about, abandoned and crucified—not only by those who hated Him, but also His closest confidants. Judas betrayed Him, Peter denied Him, and Thomas needed proof of his resurrection.

Yet in the face of unfathomable rejection, Christ died for us all. And even today, despite continual rejection, He persists in heaping blessings upon His brothers and sisters. Despite our wrongdoings, He sits at the right hand of God praying for us and pleading to God on our behalf. Therefore, let Christ be your perfect example. Because He has forgiven you of so much and continues to seek your good, return the favor to some wayward soul.

During this time of surrender, allow the Spirit to speak to you about the condition of your heart. What attitudes and beliefs does He need to rid you of in the next 31 days? The time is now; God is doing a new thing, but unforgiveness and other revenge-seeking behaviors will hinder your forward movement.

Therefore, choose the higher road—the path of love. Allow God to heal you of your hurt so that He can use you in a supernatural way in the lives of others. May God's favor be upon you today and forevermore.

#PTWG

AALIYAH'S AFFIRMATION CORNER: It's easy to love those who love me, but I look more like Jesus when I can love someone who uses me, who takes advantage of my kindness, and wishes harm upon me.

WHAT'S THIS VERSE ABOUT?
Proverbs 24:17-18

_____

_____

_____

KEEPING IT REAL: What does Christ's sacrifice mean to you?

_____

_____

_____

PRAYER CORNER: God you have called me to forgive, so please give me the strength to obey you today. Reveal any unforgiveness I am harboring in my heart and let me be free as I release others from the debt I think they owe me. These things I ask in Jesus' name. Amen.

Renewal is Necessary

But so many people were coming and going that Jesus and the apostles did not even have a chance to eat. Then Jesus said, "Let's go to a place where we can be alone and get some rest."

(Mark 6:31)

We live in a society where everyone wants to appear busy. This seems to be especially true of the DMV (the District, Maryland, and Virginia). In the last year, I have rejected the notion of busy; outright refusing to use the "b" word. Whenever someone says to me, "I know you are busy but...," I quickly correct their perception of my life informing them that I am not busy, but productive.

Some may consider this a simply matter of semantics, but to the contrary. Busy and productive are two different concepts and states of being. I have learned that "busy" is about me, while "productive" is about God.

When I am busy—for the sake of being busy, I am scattered, drained, frustrated, and inefficient. When I am productive in the things of God, I am focused, content, joyful and at peace.

That's exactly what God wants for us all. He wants us to live in the peace that surpasses all understanding, to have unspeakable joy, and to prosper in all things. If you find yourself continuously frustrated, you need to recalibrate your life and some good old-fashioned rest may be the best place to start.

You may not want to rest but it is necessary. We aren't always to be "on." Jesus understood that very well. For that reason, in Mark 6, Jesus instructed His disciples to take a break from labor. He knew that in their rest they would find renewal and the strength to be productive in the next leg of their race.

So why then do we reject rest? Pride. In fact, all busy behavior is driven by pride. Your pride drives you to believe that you can't stop, you are indispensable, and that others can't make it without you. But that is a trick of the enemy to keep you busy and unproductive. Trust me, if you died today, your friends and family would find a way to make it without you.

Therefore, I implore you to surrender your time to God and be wholly dependent on Him. Likewise, make sure the next 30 days are productive and about Him. It is in His presence that you will find the fullness of joy and rest for your soul.

#PTWG

AALIYAH'S AFFIRMATION CORNER: God wants me to have peace that surpasses all understanding, to have unspeakable joy, and to prosper in all things.

WHAT'S THIS VERSE ABOUT?
Mark 6:30-32

_____

_____

_____

KEEPING IT REAL: What is something that God wants you to eliminate? For example: a friend or a certain relationship.

_____

_____

_____

PRAYER CORNER: Dear Heavenly Father, I thank you for establishing rest as a necessary part of my existence. Help me to be mindful of its importance and to live by this standard. Not just today, but embracing rest has a habitual practice so that I can be renewed in spirit, mind, and body every day of my life. I speak this prayer by faith. Amen.

Peculiar Am I

But you are God's chosen and special people. You are
a group of royal priests and a holy nation. God has
brought you out of darkness into his marvelous light. Now
you must tell all the wonderful things that he has done.

(I Peter 2:9)

I'm different; I always have been.

In grade school my parents joined the Pentecostal
church which had certain rules. One rule was that women
couldn't wear pants. So I wore skirts from kindergarten on
into high school. In Buffalo, New York, a city known for
its terrible winters, my behavior was odd.

In college, I desperately wanted to fit in; to be "normal."
Because most of my friends cursed I thought I would try,
but when I did they asked me to stop. One friend even
declared that I was hurting his ears. What a pity, I couldn't
even curse properly.

I'm not a big medicine person because we were taught
in the Pentecostal church to pray to God for our healing.
The first time our son was sick, I prayed for his healing and
went about my business. A few hours later my husband
asked, "What did you give him for the fever?" I replied,
"I prayed." Boy, did I look strange.

I've always been told that I run funny. One day my three-year-old daughter Aaliyah challenged me to a race to the mailbox. We took off. Aaliyah, graceful and elegant, looked like a sprinter. I, in my flat-footed, pigeon-toed style of jog, looked, well, different. As we ran I heard a car approaching, I could feel them saying, "she runs funny." So what else is new? I'm different...and I'm willing to bet you are too.

But that's okay because different is good and puts us in great company. Jesus, the greatest person to ever grace this earth was also different. He was born of a virgin, lived on the wrong side of the tracks (someone was even heard saying, "Can any good think come from Nazareth?"), lacked formal education, ate with sinners, healed on the Sabbath, and died to give us life. Now if that's not different, I don't know what is. However, if He embraced His unique identity, so can we! We are a royal priesthood, a peculiar people set aside to do something great in God.

God is preparing you for your next phase in Him, but you must first accept the "you" that He has called you to be. It doesn't matter what others have said or think about you; as long as you are pleasing to God, that is all that matters. Remember, He loves you and me—peculiarities and all—just the way we are.

#PTWG

AALIYAH'S AFFIRMATION CORNER: God has great plans for my life, but I must first accept the "me" that He has called me to be.

WHAT'S THIS VERSE ABOUT?
I Peter 2:4-10

_____

_____

_____

KEEPING IT REAL: What personality trait do you find heard to accept about yourself?

_____

_____

_____

PRAYER CORNER: Dear Father in heaven, I thank you for my trials, and thank you for my tests because without them I would be incomplete. I also thank you that I am unique. Let me see how wonderfully I am made; that you didn't make a mistake, but chose me from the beginning of time. Let me walk in that truth today and set about doing exactly what it is that you have called me to do. In Jesus' name I pray. Amen.

God's Friend

I love everyone who loves me,
and I will be found by all
who honestly search.

(Proverbs 8:17)

Yesterday I had a major decision to make. Should I, or should I not continue to write for a particular magazine. I prayed about it and sensed God's answer, but still needed confirmation, so I phoned my prayer partner. We talked, and at the end of a very brief conversation she stated, "You had the answer all along."

How true were her words; *I had the answer all along.* I had prayed, God had answered yet I was doubtful.

Perhaps some of you have had a similar experience; doubting that you had heard from God when indeed you had. Or maybe you are in the habit of seeking advice from others without first seeking God's face. Whatever the case, Proverbs 8:17 offers some insight. Let's dissect it:

I love everyone who loves me,

The word "love" here comes from the Hebrew word *ahab* which means to love like a friend or ally. Of course, we know of God's agape (unconditional) love, but for Him to love us as a friend is an added benefit.

Take a moment to think about your earthly friendships. What essential qualities characterize a good friendship? Is it quality time, uncensored conversation, and/or confidence that that person has your back? Well the same should be true of your friendship with God. He doesn't just want to be your bail-out plan or the one you call when all other hope is lost. No, He desires to be your friend and connected with you in a meaningful way.

I will be found by all who honestly search.

A meaningful relationship with God includes seeking His advice first, not just when you are in trouble. Isn't it aggravating when a friend only comes to you when he/she is in need? At some point you might consider distancing yourself from him/her. But how many times have we turned to God at the end of a matter, when all (human) hope is gone? My friend that should not be so. We should be in a posture of total dependence on Him, seeking Him early for every situation. Not only early in the morning but at the beginning of the drama!

Therefore, make God your priority; seek His face, desire His presence, and become His friend. His word promises, "When you beg the Lord for help he will answer, "Here I am!" (Isaiah 58:9a).

What an awesome promise from our friend! He hears our prayer and will answer—and from now on I will trust His reply.

#PTWG

AALIYAH'S AFFIRMATION CORNER: A meaningful relationship with God includes seeking His advice first.

WHAT'S THIS VERSE ABOUT?
Proverbs 8:17

_____

_____

_____

KEEPING IT REAL: Do you know when God is speaking to you? If so, how do you know?

_____

_____

_____

PRAYER CORNER: God of the universe; God who sees all and knows all. How is it that you are mindful of me and call me friend? I am grateful for your friendship. I am grateful for your love and grateful for this time of fasting. Thank you for the changes you will make in me in the next 28 days. I surrender all. Amen.

#PTWG

Scripture(s):

How is God speaking to you today through His Word, through people, or any other way?

#PTWG

Scripture(s):

How is God speaking to you today through His Word, through people, or any other way?

I Declare War!

We are not fighting against humans. We are fighting
against forces and authorities and against rulers of
darkness and powers in the spiritual world.
(Ephesians 6:12)

As I rose from my knees this morning, the Holy Spirit
directed me to write on spiritual warfare. Little did
I know that I would have to experience it before I could post
to this blog!

Of all the things that could happen while blogging, losing
the internet connection is probably one of the worst. Well
that's just what happened. I spent over an hour booting,
rebooting, checking cords, and clicking buttons with no
success.

I wanted to give in to the frustration, but I willed my
emotions to do the opposite of my nature. So with a calm
exterior I proceeded with my morning routine: dressing the
children, dropping them off to school—all the while praying
that God would rebuke the enemy from this situation.
Thankfully, He did and I was finally able to post this blog.

What was that all about you ask? It's about the enemy
being displeased with what God is doing; about him trying

to frustrate a situation so that I will give up. But it will take a lot more than that for me to give up on God's plan for you and me.

You may be experiencing similar frustrations. Take a moment to think about what you have surrendered to God. Has the journey been easy or challenging? I would suspect that these past two weeks have been quite taxing.

Perhaps you've surrendered fear to God, yet every fear-producing situation that can happen has; maybe you're watching your words, but people and circumstances are exasperating you beyond belief; or perhaps you've committed your mornings to God only to have your alarm clock not go off. I could go on, but I think you get the picture: *there's a fight going on and we are in the middle.*

Don't be surprised when everything that could go wrong, does. The enemy, in his frustration with you, has declared all-out war, but be encouraged. The scripture reminds us that, "God's Spirit is in you and is more powerful than the one that is in the world" (I John 4:4). Accordingly, you have authority over the enemy and he has to conform to your commands.

The military has a code they use when they're on high alert. It's code red. For the next 25 days we are on high alert. Sound the alarm, there is a war going on, but with God on our side we will win!

These are the tools that you need to combat all that the enemy is sending your way:

1. **The Word** — meditate on it day and night. Commit to memory the scripture(s) that speak to your situation.
2. **Prayer** — active communication with God will strengthen your relationship with Him and allow you to feel His grace as He carries you through these challenging circumstances.
3. **Spiritual Support** — one form of spiritual support comes from this blog. But other sources of support could come from your spouse, family members, friends, and/or prayer partner(s).
4. **Self-control** — the enemy isn't interested in your comfort. He will continue to mess with you though you are frustrated, angry and/or tearful. No matter what, WILL your mind to come under subjection to the Holy Spirit. Be a good soldier and endure until the end.

Don't take Satan's tactics lying down; get on your knees and exercise the authority that Christ has given you. Say with all power, "I rebuke you in the name of Jesus" and he will flee (see James 4:7).

God placed a song in my heart this morning by Wes Morgan. When I got into my car it was playing on the radio (don't you love how God does that?). The lyrics go, "He's healing me...I'm going to worship." Rejoice today, for every crooked place God is making straight; He is making a way in the wilderness and rivers in deserts.

Nonetheless, the enemy is displeased, so suit up. There is a war going on and with God we will win!

#PTWG

AALIYAH'S AFFIRMATION CORNER: I won't let the devil walk all over me. I am going to pray and use the power that God has given me to defeat Him.

WHAT'S THIS VERSE ABOUT?
Ephesians 6:12

_____

_____

_____

KEEPING IT REAL: When you have an issue, do you go to God first or to family and friends?

_____

_____

_____

PRAYER CORNER: Lord thank you for the strategy that you have given us in prayer. Thank you Lord that this war the enemy has waged is already won. Let me be courageous; let me fight by faith knowing that you are with me and because of that, I am more than victorious. In Jesus' name I pray. Amen.

Superhuman

But those who trust the Lord
will find new strength.
They will be strong like eagles
soaring upward on wings;
they will walk and run
without getting tired.

(Isaiah 40:31)

The other day I was watching Stan Lee's *Superhumans* on the History Channel. The title is self-descriptive. Each episode features people who do amazing feats that defy nature. The particular show I watched featured a gentleman that could run and never tire. The show's scientist soon discovered why. Lactic acid, the chemical released in the body during strenuous exercise that leads to fatigue, remained at low levels in his body at all times. For this reason, he was deemed a superhuman.

The strength this man exhibited in his natural body is akin to the strength that we, who are in Christ, can access in the spirit. In God we are super humans. His word confirms this truth. The Prophet Isaiah wrote we shall run and not grow weary, walk and not faint.

One way this superhuman strength is acquired is through the process of waiting. *"What?! You might ask. Simply waiting?"* Trust me, there is nothing simple about waiting; it defies our nature. The flesh wants everything right now, this instant. However, it is said that anything worth having, is worth waiting for, and God's blessings are certainly worth the wait.

I remember the day that I was accepted to the University of Pittsburgh for their doctorate program. I was super excited. The phone call from the faculty member started well, but soon took a sour turn when he shared with me that the program didn't have the funds to allow me to attend for free which had been one of my stipulations. I was disappointed, but unwilling to compromise because God had told me that He would fully fund this leg of my education. So I boldly told him that I would have to decline admittance unless they found me funding. Then I waited.

The wait wasn't easy. Several times I was tempted to call them back and accept the offer without funding. But each time I felt that way, I prayed, and God renewed my strength. Three weeks later I received the phone call I had been waiting for. They had found enough money to fund my entire doctorate degree! Because I trusted in God's promises and waited, I was rewarded.

Stop trying to make things happen in your own strength. If God said it, He will do it. Isaiah 55:11 reads, "That's how it is with my words. They don't return to me without doing everything I send them to do."

If you are waiting on God for a promotion...wait; a husband...wait; a new job...wait; acceptance into a program...wait. Although everything around you may be falling apart and things aren't going the way you planned, He is in control and will work it out in due time.

Therefore, I declare that you, too, can be super human if you simply wait on God and let His supernatural power work in your life.

#PTWG

------o------○------o------

AALIYAH'S AFFIRMATION CORNER: Today I declare that I can be super human if I simply wait on God and let His supernatural power work in my life.

WHAT'S THIS VERSE ABOUT?
Isaiah 40:31

_____

_____

_____

KEEPING IT REAL: Do you believe that God gives you power over the enemy?

_____

_____

_____

PRAYER CORNER: Dear Heavenly Father, thank you for your patience and for giving me a mind to wait on your will. Lord you have given me free will and you allow me to do what I care to do, but Lord I don't want to do it that way anymore. I want to be surrendered to your will. So Lord give me a mind to wait because as I wait, your will is done and I reap an abundant harvest. I ask these things in the mighty name of Jesus. Amen.

The God in Me

The chest stayed there for three months, and the Lord
greatly blessed Obed Edom, his family, and everything
he owned.

(II Samuel 6:11)

Have you ever wondered why you are where you are?
Why God has placed you at a certain job, church,
community group, school, or even family? I certainly have.

I remember once working a job that I hated. I was
miserable and made sure that God (and even those I worked
with) knew it. I prayed that He would move me, but my
prayers seemed to fall on deaf ears. What I didn't understand
then, was that God had a plan. He needed me there and He
wasn't going to move me until His plans had been fulfilled.

Since that time, I have learned to recognize God's
sovereign hand in all of my situations. A story that reminds
me of the importance of doing this, is told in II Samuel
6. As the story goes, David and the children of Israel
had been in the process of transporting the Ark of God
to the city of Jerusalem, when tragedy stuck. One of their
own, Uzzah, was killed by God when he touched the ark.
David, deeply troubled by this occurrence, aborted the

transporting mission. He then left the ark in the home of Obed-Edom, the brother of the deceased.

I can only imagine Obed-Edom's "delight" to have the ark that had killed his brother, reside in his home. He may have wondered if he would face the same fate or he may have longed to be free from the obligation of housing the ark. However, God wasn't moving the ark until He was ready. What Obed-Edom failed to realize was that God's presence always brings blessings. For the three months that the ark remained with Obed-Edom, he and his entire household were blessed.

This story has huge implications for how we are to approach life today. Just like Obed-Edom, we will be called to seasons we don't want to weather or like the ark be placed in situations where we are unwanted. There will also be times when we will be despised and rejected because of the God in us. Nonetheless, if we keep the faith and trust in God's plan, those around us will be blessed. Not because we are so good, but because God's presence resides in us. His word reads, "the Lord's Spirit sets us free" (2 Corinthians 3:17). Therefore, those in direct contact with us should feel His presence and find rest.

In light of this truth, stop fighting God's plan and complaining about your station in life. You may not understand it all now, but He does, so trust that He has a plan and that it will work out for your good. If you are willing to endure a little discomfort for a season, others will have the awesome opportunity to see God in you and be blessed beyond measure.

#PTWG

AALIYAH'S AFFIRMATION CORNER: If I'm willing to be uncomfortable for a little while, others will have the opportunity to see God in me and be blessed beyond measure.

WHAT'S THIS VERSE ABOUT?
II Samuel 6:11

_____
_____
_____

KEEPING IT REAL: Do you wait for God to do His work or do you want everything right now?

_____
_____
_____

PRAYER CORNER: God I may not be where I want to be, but I trust that I am where I need to be in order for your will to be done. Thank you for this opportunity. I will allow you to maximize your presence through me with no complaints. I surrender all to you. In Jesus' name I pray. Amen.

The Keys for Good Relationships

It is truly wonderful
when relatives live together in peace.
(Psalm 133:1)

Unless you live on a deserted island, you are in relationship with at least one other person. For some this is easy—he/she finds freedom in being in relationship with others—while for others, relationships are challenging to say the least.

God emphasizes numerous times in scripture the importance of being in unity with others. He knows that healthy vibrant living is contingent on the quality of our relationships. Research indicates this is especially true of women; love is everything in the life of a woman. For her, the lack of healthy, thriving relationships can lead to depression, anxiety and other psychological problems. This fact of life confirms that God designed us to be in healthy relationships and to dwell in unity. You can only do this when you don't gossip about the other person, but go directly to them to resolve the issue. Sometimes that is not possible and that is okay.

Lastly, make up your mind today to dwell in unity in all your relationships; it will serve you well. If you have a relationship in need of repair, ask the Holy Spirit to give you the words to speak so that the conflict is resolved. If your efforts don't work and you believe that the relationship is worth saving, find a "neutral" third party to help the two of you resolve your conflict. It will be worth the effort because obeying God's word in this matter will allow you to reap the benefits (e.g., peace, joy, etc.) of dwelling in peace-filled, unified relationships.

#PTWG

AALIYAH'S AFFIRMATION CORNER: God designed me to be in healthy relationships and to be in unity with other people.

WHAT'S THIS VERSE ABOUT?
Psalm 133

_____

_____

_____

KEEPING IT REAL: Is everything okay right now? If not, explain your situation.

_____

_____

_____

PRAYER CORNER: Lord your holy scripture calls me to dwell in unity, to do what is in my power to live peaceably and to show myself friendly. I vow to do that today. Also, strengthen the relationships I have and show me the people that I need to reach out to; to either apologize or reconcile the relationship in some other way. In Jesus' name I pray. Amen.

I Still Surrender

Our people defeated Satan
because of the blood of the Lamb
and the message of God.
(Revelation 12:11a)

We are nearly 50% of the way there. How are you faring? My experience with this fast gives me insight to where you might be in the process. Right about now, if you have committed your all to this fast, the surrender may seem as if it will overwhelm you. For example, if you surrendered "fear," you may feel consumed by it; if "control," everything may be falling apart; or if "spending more time with your children," every distraction that can come has.

To make matters worse, the enemy is probably bombarding you with every negative thought and circumstance he can drum up to get you to give up or start over—but don't. Persist through the pressure; you are nearly to the finish line. I assure you that somewhere around Day 28, or soon thereafter, you will start to feel a release. So hold on.

Tomorrow, I will have my next big, bold, and courageous moment. I am speaking to a group of 9th—12th grade girls at a women's conference with over 4,000 participants.

"What's so challenging about that?" you might ask. Everything. Let me testify so that I can overcome by my words.

First, I am self-conscious around large groups of women. Secondly, God has instructed me to attend the conference without wearing makeup (specifically foundation). You would have to know my story to understand how women and makeup go together.

In a nutshell, as a teen I wasn't accepted by the girls that I thought mattered. As a result, I concluded that there was something wrong with me. I was just too different: I didn't talk or think like the other girls, I wore skirts all the time, and I had acne. Therefore, as an adult I worked really hard on projecting the perfect image. So I began my love affair with makeup.

Oh yes, it has been a love affair. In fact, God told me it was an idol. Accordingly, He suggested in June of 2010 that I present at the Regional Lady of Virtue Conference in Buffalo, New York, without it. I fought God on His suggestion, but He knew, as well as I, that He would win, because I love and trust Him, and (nearly) always comply with His requests.

Since that conference I haven't gone back to wearing the foundation. Not that it's wrong, just wrong for me right now. So when they announced that I would be one of the speakers at the First Baptist Church of Glenarden Women's Conference, I panicked. Me and 4,000 strange women who could reject me? No way. *I would definitely need to order some foundation*, I thought. Instantly the Holy Spirit forbade it. We literally argued back and forth, but with tears streaming down my face I decided to comply. I would not wear foundation to the conference.

That might seem small to you, but for me it's major, bold and courageous, and crazy. But I am okay with that because at the end of this fast it will be worth it. I will obtain the ultimate prize: *freedom from every thought and pattern of living that keeps me from living a victorious life*. Now, that, my friend, is well worth fighting for.

Your surrender is equally as important. You will be the victor if you faint not. You are almost to the finish line; be sure to see it through to the end.

#PTWG

AALIYAH'S AFFIRMATION CORNER: I will be the victor if I faint not. I'm almost to the finish line; I'll see it through to the end.

WHAT'S THIS VERSE ABOUT?
Revelation 12:11a

_____

_____

_____

KEEPING IT REAL: Are you ready to surrender to God or is something holding you back? Explain.

_____

_____

_____

PRAYER CORNER: God help me to know that surrender is the only option now and for always. No matter what has occurred in the last 19 days, or will occur in the next 21, let it not be enough to turn me back around. For indeed, I've come too far to turn back now. Let me keep my eyes on you and have a glorious finish to this amazing journey. In Jesus' name I pray. Amen

#PTWG

Scripture(s):

How is God speaking to you today through His Word, through people, or any other way?

#PTWG

Scripture(s):

How is God speaking to you today through His Word, through people, or any other way?

Dust off Your Dreams

If you keep thinking about something, you will dream
about it.
If you talk too much, you will say the wrong thing.
(Ecclesiastes 5:3)

As mentioned in the previous post, I had the pleasure of ministering to 9th-12th grade girls at the First Baptist Church of Glenarden Women's Conference this past weekend. What a blessed time we had in the Lord! God's agenda was clear: *the girls are to dream big, dream bold, and always remember that He does not forget.* He reminded them that when He plants a dream in the heart, it comes to pass. That truth is confirmed in Habakkuk 2: 2-3.
Then the LORD told me:
> "I will give you my message
> in the form of a vision.
> Write it clearly enough
> to be read at a glance.
> At the time I have decided,
> my words will come true.
> You can trust what I say
> about the future.
> It may take a long time,

but keep on waiting—
it will happen!

In the 7th grade, God planted a dream in my heart during 4th period study hall. While browsing the microfiche in the library, I happened to come upon an article about a little boy who was killed by his mother. The story deeply troubled my spirit and it was in that instant God revealed to me part of His plan for my life. I knew then that I would be a psychologist.

The journey towards that dream was difficult. I had to fight for college funding, endure prejudice, and live meagerly. Nonetheless, His plan for my life came to pass in 2002 when I obtained my doctorate degree. I am now a psychologist.

Over the years, God has planted many more dreams in my heart. Some have come to pass while others tarry. Am I worried? Not a bit. They too will come to pass if I wait on the Lord.

What are the dreams that God has planted in you? Well now is the time to dust them off, put them back on your agenda, and pursue them as God leads you. Don't get overly concerned with the details. Les Brown, motivational speaker, says "the *how* is none of your business." Trust that God has it all handled and He will provide the means. All He needs from you is your willingness to comply with His every command.

Research indicates that those who write down their dreams are substantially more likely to pursue and achieve them, than those who do not. Therefore, I encourage you to write out each and every one of your dreams today. Then place them in a place where you can see them on the run or as you go about your daily activities. Let them be a constant reminder of what God has promised. It's never too late...though the vision tarries it's only for a while, He will do just as He said.

Let me give you a quick word of caution. Be sure the dreams that you are pursuing are God's and not yours. Our flesh can get in the way and encourage us to pursue a dream that is not a part of God's plan for our lives. If you are unsure, pray to God for wisdom. Then ask Him to confirm His truth to you either through His word and/or godly people. When the dream is confirmed, believe that it will come to pass no matter what life brings your way.

Lastly, though a dream comes with much business and painful effort, the pursuit of a godly dream is well worth the fight. Be encouraged my sisters and brothers. God is not through with you yet and His dreams will come to pass!

#PTWG

AALLIYAH SPEAKS: Trust that God has it all handled and He will give you everything you need to make your dreams come true.

WHAT'S THIS VERSE ABOUT?
Ecclesiastes 5:3

_____

_____

_____

KEEPING IT REAL: Have you been tempted to give up on this fast? If so, what is the issue?

_____

_____

_____

PRAYER CORNER: Dear Heavenly Father, you have planted dreams in my heart. Encourage me to re-visit those dreams today. If the passion is gone, cause me to dream again. And I invite you to place new dreams in my heart. Let them know that you are not through with me yet and your dreams will come to pass. In Jesus' name I pray. Amen

Your Breakthrough is Coming Through

Right away his hand went back in, and the other child was born first. The woman then said, "What an opening you've made for yourself!" So they named the baby Perez

(Genesis 38:29)

T here is a story in the Bible that has fascinated me for years. It comes from a chapter in the book of Genesis. I hadn't read it in a while, but this morning God spoke to me "Genesis 38." Honestly, I couldn't remember what Genesis 38 pertained to, but when I opened my Bible to this passage of scripture, I knew. This was the story of the breakthrough.

Genesis 38 features Judah, the son of Jacob and brother to Joseph. As the story goes, Judah and his other brothers were very jealous of Joseph because of the love Jacob had for his son. Their hatred of Joseph led them to plot a scheme to rid themselves of him. As a result, he was sold into slavery.

Soon after this occurrence, Judah left home and moved in with his friend Hirah at Adullam. There, Judah met a woman, took her as his wife, and she bore him 3 sons:

Er, Onan, and Shelah. When his eldest son Er was of age he married Tamar. Unfortunately, Er was evil in the sight of the Lord and He killed him.

His death left Tamar a widow, but not really. According to their custom, Onan, the second son was to take Tamar as his wife and raise offspring for his brother. Onan, not "feeling" his fate, prevented conception. This displeased the Lord, so He killed him.

Poor Tamar. Two husbands dead and still no heir. But there was one last hope: Shelah. Accordingly, Judah instructed Tamar to remain a widow in her father's house until Shelah came of age. Unfortunately, Judah had decided in his heart, now considering Tamar a jinx, that she would never have this son and with that her fate was sealed...or so he thought. He had underestimated Tamar. She wouldn't take this course of action lying down; she had a plan.

When Tamar learned that Judah was visiting Timnath to shear his sheep, she pretended to be a harlot. Judah took the bait, and subsequently impregnated her. Some months later when he learned of her pregnancy, he ordered that she be stoned. However, when Tamar proved to him that he was the father, he proclaimed to all that were listening, "She has been more righteous than I, because I did not give her to Shelah my son."

Wow, total vindication. But the story doesn't end there. Tamar's "power move" landed her in the genealogy hall of fame. The son she bore, ironically named Perez which means breakthrough, carried on the messianic line until the time of David, and ultimately to Jesus. Matthew 1:3a reads, "Judah's sons were Perez and Zerah, and their mother was Tamar."

What an amazing turn of events. This woman, who had to pretend to be a harlot to get her father-in-law to do right by her, gives birth to a child who is a descendent for our Lord and Savior! What a comeback.

Like Tamar, we've all been hurt by other people or victim to situations that were out of our control. Yet her story demonstrates the importance of allowing God to work things out. We certainly don't have to take the enemy's tactics lying down. Discouragement, fear, doubt, and guilt are from him, but with the power of God working in us, we can do something about our dead situations and change the course of our lives.

You may have been discounted, but that doesn't have to be your fate. You are in and not out, the victor and not the conquered, the head and not the tail, above and not beneath (see Deuteronomy 28). In Jesus' name your breakthrough is coming through and destined to arrive within the next 17 days. Stay strong in your faith, trust God and watch him orchestrate a comeback that will give Him all the glory.

#PTWG

AALIYAH'S AFFIRMATION CORNER: I am the victor and not the conquered, the head and not the tail, above and not beneath.

WHAT'S THIS VERSE ABOUT?
Genesis 38:29

_____

_____

_____

KEEPING IT REAL: What are your dreams? Write them here or on another paper.

_____

_____

_____

PRAYER CORNER: God of the universe; You are greatly to be praised. Thank you for being mindful of me and working on my behalf even when it doesn't appear that anything is happening on the surface. Thank you that on this Day 23 I am reminded that my breakthrough is coming through. Let me be patient, and trust your timing because before I know it, it will happen. In Jesus' name I pray. Amen

The Answered Prayer

Eli replied, "You may go home now and stop worrying.
I'm sure the God of Israel will answer your prayer."
(I Samuel 1:17)

During the course of this fast, you have petitioned God with specific requests, not only praying for your own deliverance, but interceding and seeking God on behalf of your family and friends. Today, God has sent me to tell you that He hears you. Your prayers have not gone unheard, nor your surrender unnoticed, and many people will be blessed because of your sacrifice.

This morning as I prayed for my brother's salvation and for one marriage in particular, God led me to I Samuel 1:17. It reads, "Eli replied, "You may go home now and stop worrying. I'm sure the God of Israel will answer your prayer."

This is one of my favorite phrases in the Bible as it helped me through a challenging season in my life. My first pregnancy ended in a miscarriage and it was devastating. After that occurrence, I was bombarded with negative thoughts: *Was I too old? Would I be able to conceive and carry a baby full-term? Was this punishment for some past sin?* And as the fear grew, the questions increased.

In a quest for peace, I turned to God's word and He directed me to the Book of 1 Samuel. The first few chapters feature the story of Hannah, a barren woman who desperately desired a son. So with a pure heart she cried out for God's help and He complied. By way of confirmation, Eli the priest spoke to her the scripture you read above (I Samuel 1:17). Those words were a huge source of comfort for Hannah and should be for us today.

The Word also tells us, *"The Lord watches over everyone who obeys him, and he listens to their prayers. But he opposes everyone who does evil"* (1 Peter 3:12). Praise God! He hears our prayers and is ready to answer. What are you seeking God for? Ask in faith, according to His will, and it is done.

How do I know? Has He not requested that we *Let Him Do a New Thing*, and declared that we are to *Expect the Unexpected?* Has He not proclaimed that *It Will Come to Pass*, and that *Your Breakthrough is Coming Through?* What more can He say? As the prophet Eli instructed Hannah, "Go in peace." In other words, be content with today, praise God for what He has already done, and wait expectantly, without worry, for what is to come.

Therefore, I am resting in the promises of God. I praise Him for my brother's salvation and the marriages that will be restored. I thank Him that I will be all that He has proclaimed within the next 16 days and the same can be true for you. Don't fret; it is already done, go in peace.

#PTWG

AALIYAH'S AFFIRMATION CORNER: I'll be content with today, praise God for what He has already done, and wait expectantly, without worry, for what is to come.

WHAT'S THIS VERSE ABOUT?
I Samuel 1:17

_____

_____

_____

KEEPING IT REAL: Are you in need of God's help? If so, do you think he will help you?

_____

_____

_____

PRAYER CORNER: Dear Heavenly Father, thank you for being an on-time God. Thank you for answering my prayers. Perhaps more importantly, thank you for giving me the grace to wait, because indeed your timing is perfect. These things we ask in the matchless name of Jesus. Amen.

The Dead Will Live

Jesus heard what they said, and he said to Jairus,
"Don't worry. Just have faith!"
(Mark 5:36)

I can recall as a child hearing a preacher tell one unbelievable story of how he had been raised from the dead. Yes, you read correctly, raised from the dead.

This preacher was a sight to behold: tall, dark, and disfigured. His deformity, the result of a fire, had burned him across most of his body and subsequently killed him.

As a matter of fact, that would have been the end of the story, but God. Fortunately for him, there were many saints praying on his behalf. As a result of their prayers, he woke up in the morgue, naked, with a tag on his toe. Can you imagine the surprise, to put it mildly, of the attendant on duty that night?

In Jesus' day, a ruler of the synagogue came to Him by the name of Jairus. He prostrated himself at His feet, and begged that He come to lay hands on his little girl that was dying. Jesus agreed. Yet as they traveled, there were many distractions: the crowd, the woman with the issue of blood, and no doubt other requests of Jesus.

In no time, a servant reported that Jairus' daughter had died and that he should "cease from bothering and distressing the Teacher." For most people that would have been the end of the story: she's dead, it's over. But as the song reminds us, "It ain't over, until God says it's over; He has the final say."

So the story continued. Jesus, having overheard the conversation between the ruler and his servant simply responded, "Don't worry. Just have faith!" (Mark 5:36). With that, Jesus continued to Jairus' home, spoke to the little girl, and she lived.

What is your response to "dead" situations? Do you throw your hands up, give in to the fear, and wallow in disappointment? Or do you pursue, with power, all that has been stolen from you? I pray it is the latter.

My friend, if God has spoken a thing to you in the spirit and your natural circumstances don't line up, so what! It's not over. Don't give in to the fear and don't give up. Instead, pray with all your might, and praise God for what He has already done. The Word tells us to speak those things that are not as though they were so (see Romans 4:17). This is not the time for giving up, but for establishing your faith.

Is there anyone better to put your faith in than Jesus? He, too, gave life to a dead situation. He was crucified, buried, and in three days resurrected. That miracle testifies to us today that our dead situations can also live if we only believe.

Rejoice because God has promised that he will restore the years that the locust has eaten—and that you, His people, will never be put to shame (see Joel 2:25-26). Therefore, in the next 15 days, let God resurrect and bring life to your dead situations.

#PTWG

---○---

AALIYAH'S AFFIRMATION CORNER: It ain't over, until God says it's over. He has the final say.

WHAT'S THIS VERSE ABOUT?
Mark 5:36

_____

_____

_____

KEEPING IT REAL: How are your thoughts? Do you let the enemy get in your head or do you keep in positive?

_____

_____

_____

PRAYER CORNER: I am grateful that You are the God of the resurrection; nothing is impossible for you. So for that reason and many more, I trust you. I believe and won't be afraid. Do with my life as you please, and resurrect the people, circumstances and situations needed to move me into Your next. In Jesus' name I pray. Amen.

What is For Me is For Me

They are like trees growing beside a stream,
trees that produce fruit in season and always have leaves.
Those people succeed in everything they do.
(Psalm 1:3)

I was visiting a colleague's website last night and noticed that she had been asked to speak at a major event on the east coast. I immediately went to the event's webpage to see who else had been asked to speak. As I perused the site my mind started to spin; doubt threatened to consume me as one fear-based thought led to another. My train of thought went something like this:

Why wasn't I asked to speak? Because they don't know me; they don't know me because I am not connected to the right people; but how does one connect with the right people? Perhaps if I was little less Bible-based; maybe if I watered the message down and made it more universally acceptable; yes, I better change, otherwise I will never build a speaking platform and worse yet, life will pass me by.

Just thoughts, or are they? If they were *just* thoughts, then the scripture that directs us to bring "we capture people's thoughts and make them obey Christ." would be unnecessary (2 Corinthians 10:5b). Our thoughts have power and if we linger on them long enough they'll direct our actions.

Therefore, as the thoughts attempted to bombard me, I did what I knew would bring relief—I fell on my knees and prayed to God for strength to challenge my thoughts. In an instant He comforted me with these words:

You can't miss out on what I have for you.

Those were the exact words that my prayer partner had spoken to me a few months prior and they brought me great comfort as I was reminded that *I can't miss out on what God has for me.*

The scripture tells us that if you do what the Lord wants, He will make certain each step you take is sure (see Psalm 37:23). Because I am righteous (in right standing with God), habitually meditating on His word, and delighting myself in Him, I can't miss out! As the song goes, "What God has for me it is for me." Likewise, if you are in God's will, you can't miss out either. If He said it, it is so; His word will not return to Him void and it will achieve the purposes for which it was sent (see Isaiah 55:11).

Therefore, when in despair, cling to these scriptures as your truth: "Do what the Lord wants, and he will give you your heart's desire" (Psalm 37:4) ; and "Always obey them [God's laws and teachings], and the Lord will make Israel the most famous and important nation on earth, and he will bless you in many ways" (Deuteronomy 28:1-2). As my Auntie Gwen would say, "Those are words to live by."

Don't measure your life by the world's standards; don't let their timetables convince you that you are doing something wrong. God's timing is perfect and if you are walking in His will, He will bring forth the fruit of your labor in its season. I don't know about you, but I don't want what God hasn't ordained. While it might look good to the world its end is destruction.

Therefore, I praise God for reminding me and you that when we walk according to His plan we can't miss out. We can't miss connecting with the right people, finding the perfect job, being appointed over a ministry, elected into political office, finding the right mate, becoming a homeowner, or having children. Indeed, what He has for me is for me and what He has for you is for you. Be encouraged!

#PTWG

AALIYAH'S AFFIRMATION CORNER: When I walk according to God's plan, I can't miss out.

WHAT'S THIS VERSE ABOUT?
Psalm 1:3, 37:4, 23

_____

_____

_____

KEEPING IT REAL: Do you get jealous of other people when they get something that you want? Why or why not?

_____

_____

_____

PRAYER CORNER: Lord I thank you for closed doors because I know that if you closed one door, you can open another. Let me trust you with all my heart and lean not to my own understanding. And let me not forget that what is for me, is for me and it will make its way to me in due time. In Jesus' name I pray. Amen.

#PTWG

Scripture(s):

How is God speaking to you today through His Word, through people, or any other way?

#PTWG

Scripture(s):

How is God speaking to you today through His Word, through people, or any other way?

The God of the Impossible

Jesus looked straight at them and said, "There are
some things that people cannot do,
but God can do anything."
(Matthew 19:26)

I have the ultimate praise report today! My brother, who I had declared would accept Christ as his personal savior before the conclusion of this fast, did. Yesterday, before hundreds of witnesses at my father's 10th Pastoral Anniversary Celebration in Lockport, New York, he received the gift of eternal salvation.

That is no small feat; God did the miraculous. My brother Stephen, age 27 and the youngest of us eight, was a tough sell; he didn't appear to have any interest in salvation. The rest of us had been saved for years, but not Stephen. He was content, or so he thought, to live his life in sin. But God always has the final say and He honors the prayers of His people.

I was later told that during the anniversary service my mother stood boldly before the people and announced that all of her children were saved. Stephen, sitting in the audience, probably thought, *you forgot about me,* but she hadn't. At that moment she was simply establishing her faith and God did the seemingly impossible in a matter of minutes.

How many times has God told you that He was going to move on your behalf or the behalf of your family and instead of proclaiming His declaration aloud, you sit on it till the enemy has convinced you otherwise? Certainly, the scripture tells us there are times to have faith to ourselves but this is not for every instance. Sometimes God wants you to act in boldness and declare His promises aloud so that others will witness His mighty hand in your situation and also believe.

In this season, God is calling us to a level of radical faith that far exceeds our previous dealings with Him. He wants us to know that if He could part the Red Sea, feed 5,000 with two fish and five loaves of bread, and raise Jesus from the dead that He can *and* will move in our situations.

Will you not believe in Him today? He declares, "If you had faith no bigger than a tiny mustard seed, you could tell this mulberry tree to pull itself up, roots and all, and to plant itself in the ocean. And it would!" (Luke 17:6). Another scripture reads, "Ask me, and I will do whatever you ask. This way the Son will bring honor to the Father. I will do whatever you ask me to do." (John 14:13-14).

I encourage you to pray, hear from God, and with holy boldness declare the humanly impossible. Some of you need college tuition, a wayward spouse to return home, a child to come off drugs, a spouse, promotion, new home, car, and/ or God's peace; whatever it is, ask and BELIEVE. Better yet, why not DECLARE what God will do by sharing your belief with your accountability partner? Go ahead, you can do it! Act in faith and watch Him do beyond what you could ask or think. If He did it for us by saving our brother, He will also do it for you. Let it all be done in Jesus' Name!

#PTWG

---•---

AALIYAH'S AFFIRMATION CORNER: In this season, God is calling me to a level of radical faith like I never demonstrated before. I will show God that I trust Him.

WHAT'S THIS VERSE ABOUT?
Matthew 19:26

_____

_____

_____

KEEPING IT REAL: Are you currently in a tough time in your life? If so, do you believe that God can get you out?

_____

_____

_____

PRAYER CORNER: Dear Heavenly Father, thank you for your love, protection, and divine timing. Thank you that every request I have made according to your will, shall come to pass. Help me to keep the faith Lord, and help me to have unwaveringly belief in you and your ability to perform. I ask these things in the matchless name of Jesus the Christ. Amen.

Little Time Needed

The Lord says:
"My thoughts and my ways are not like yours.
(Isaiah 55:8)

oday was unusual. I couldn't seem to get my thoughts together. I would start a blog post only to delete and start over. With each passing minute my anxiety grew. I feared that I wouldn't have time to write something meaningful. It was in that moment that the Holy Spirit whispered these profound words, "*God doesn't need a lot of time.*" Take a moment and let that permeate into your being.

God doesn't need a lot of time.

Yesterday, God asked us to declare in faith, and according to His will, what He will do for us; how He will bless us as a reward for our sacrifice. Some of you flat out refused. You weren't willing to put yourself "out there."

Although God has declared *new things* and for you to *expect the unexpected*, some of you continue to believe that these promises are for everyone else but you. Indeed, for some of you that has been the story of your life: left out, forgotten, and rejected, but not this time. Can He do it for you? Yes, He can! And He will in just 11 more days, if you step out in faith.

When I first started writing this blog, I wanted the posts to follow a succinct pattern. If I would have had my way, each week would have covered a specific theme (e.g., Week 1-Fear; Week 2 — Self-esteem, etc.). But thank God He had another plan. As we are nearing the end, I realize that He has used this time to simply build our faith in Him.

The scripture reads in Jeremiah 17:5, "I, the Lord, have put a curse on those who turn from me and trust in human strength." We have learned and are continuing to learn, that our trust is to be in God, and Him alone; not other people or our own abilities. The latter is weak and leads to our doom, but when we trust in God, we trust in the source of all goodness and our success is guaranteed. He will do just as He said, in the amount of time that He chooses.

So let's start over. What has God declared that He will do for you by the conclusion of this fast? Then it is done. It is often for the building of your faith that He allows you to wait until His appointed time. Therefore, don't look at your circumstances; just keep your eyes on God. I don't care if you are in the 11th hour, if He said He will do it, it is done. Remember, He doesn't need a lot of time so simply believe and receive your inheritance.

#PTWG

AALIYAH'S AFFIRMATION CORNER: God doesn't need a lot of time.

WHAT'S THIS VERSE ABOUT?
Isaiah 55:8

_____
_____
_____

KEEPING IT REAL: God can do anything at any time. Do you believe that although God doesn't do something right away that it will still happen?

_____
_____
_____

PRAYER CORNER: God thank for the grace to wait on you and to trust your timing. You will do what you have said, in the amount of time you chose and I am okay with that. I believe in you and trust in you with all my heart. Thank you for being God. Thank you for blessing me. In Jesus' Name I pray. Amen.

Grace and Glory

You were saved by faith in God, who treats us much better than we deserve. This is God's gift to you, and not anything you have done on your own. It isn't something you have earned, so there is nothing you can brag about.

(Ephesians 2:8-9)

We are in the last quarter of this race. I pray that you remain focused so that you are able to win and receive all that God has for you!

Last night in Bible Study the praise team sang a song that continues to permeate my spirit. The lyrics, *"All the glory belongs to you, All the glory belongs to you, O God"* are on my lips even this morning. For indeed, all the glory belongs to God for what He has done and will do.

I am specifically praising God this morning for His grace. Grace is God's unmerited favor and the power to do what we can't do in our own strength. When we accepted Christ as our personal savior, it was God's grace that made it possible. The writer Paul wrote:

"But God was merciful! We were dead because of our sins, but God loved us so much that he made us alive with Christ, and God's wonderful kindness is what saves you." (Ephesians 2:4-5).

Without God's grace we would still be dead in our sins, wallowing in a sea of defeat and desperation.

So why then as believers are we living in a state of virtual gracelessness; not allowing Him to work on our behalf? Indeed, if we needed Him then (to receive the gift of salvation), we need Him now. It is only by His grace that we will accomplish what He wills for our lives and succeed.

I told you in a former post that I was uncomfortable with writing. So when God called me to blog, I knew I needed His grace and power to do what was outside of my skill-set and comfort level. Therefore, each morning I submit to His plan, listen for what He has to say, and write as He instructs. And look what He has done! Many of you (including readers from 10 different countries) have been blessed by God's grace operating in my life.

I sense that some of you are working too hard for God's dream. He has promised you "X" and before He can work on your behalf, you are making futile efforts to make it so. God doesn't need your help; it is not by your works that His will comes to pass, but His grace. I heard Pastor Paul Sheppard say, "When we fight, God doesn't." This isn't to imply that we are to live passively, it's simply a reminder that God is in control and we are to move only as He leads.

Therefore, if God has promised to save your son, stop lecturing him. If God has promised to bring your husband into right fellowship with Him, stop criticizing him. If God has promised to give you a new car; don't settle for a used one. Stand on His word, get out of the way, and let Him work!

Indeed, God will do a great work by this fast's end and His grace will allow His every promise to come true for you. If your faith is lacking, re-read the post entitled, *Rebuild and Renew*. It reminds you that God is looking to bless you and your families outrageously as a result of your sacrifice. All He needs for you to do is to believe and let His grace flow.

Take courage. Speak aloud what God has promised He will do. If you don't know what that is, ask. The scripture reads, "If any of you need wisdom, you should ask God, and it will be given to you. God is generous and won't correct you for asking" (James 1:5). And when He gives you His plan, believe it. Refrain from planning how you will make it happen; simply let His grace and His power direct your every step.

To God be the glory. I can't wait to hear the testimonies of how His grace empowered you to do what you were unable to do in your own strength; how your surrender has made the impossible, possible.

Now sing with me, "All the glory belongs to you, All the glory belongs to you, O God."

#PTWG

AALIYAH'S AFFIRMATION CORNER: With God nothing is impossible!

WHAT'S THIS VERSE ABOUT?
Ephesians 2:8-9

_____

_____

_____

KEEPING IT REAL: Are you doing God's will now? If you aren't, what is holding you back?

_____

_____

_____

PRAYER CORNER: Thank you God for your grace; without it I would be nothing. Whatever you have called me to, give me the grace to complete it. And not only that, to excel in such a way that you will get all the glory. In Jesus' Name I pray. Amen.

Act Like You Are About To Move

To go through the camp and tell everyone:
In a few days we will cross the Jordan River to take the
land that the Lord our God is giving us. So fix as much
food as you'll need for the march into the land.
(Joshua 1:11)

There was a message preached by Pastor John K.
Jenkins, Sr. of the First Baptist Church of Glenarden
that left a lasting impression on me. Ironically, I can't recall
the theme of the message or even the sermon title but one
key point stuck out for me. He said that faith is active and
when God has spoken a word in your life, act as if it is
already done.

I was speaking with a sister who shared with me that
God has promised her a new home at a specific address.
I readily replied, "start acting like you are about to move."
My instructions to her included:

1. **Purge the junk.** Throw out those things that are not
   suitable for your new dwelling place.
2. **Scout out the land.** Go to the new address and
   pray over your new home and neighborhood.

3. Prepare for transport. Phone moving companies, compare rates, and decide which company to use.

In other words, ACT LIKE YOU ARE ABOUT TO MOVE.

If God has promised you a new car, start visiting dealerships to learn everything there is to know about the car buying process. If God has promised to send you to school, start scouting the local colleges; learn which have your major, and who will fund you. If God has promised you a promotion, learn all that you need to know about your next position. If God has promised you a husband, get out the house and move in circles that are husband-friendly so he can find you!

In other words, ACT LIKE YOU ARE ABOUT TO MOVE.

There is a period of time late in a woman's pregnancy where she actively prepares for her baby's arrival. No matter how long her journey or how challenging the pregnancy, every expectant mother comes to this stage. It's called Nesting. It is in this stage that she finds renewed energy and strength to prepare for her impending blessing. In fact, it has been reported that nurseries have been completed in a day by the pregnant woman alone! In that instance she was acting like she was about to move.

Lately, I've been hearing the words, *start acting like you are a business.* Although everything around me doesn't look like a business (e.g., I am still typing a blog from my family room), I am heeding these words. Accordingly, I have contacted a web designer, researched speaker agents, and developed a plan for hiring staff. Hey, it may not look like it right now but I am giving birth to an international ministry of ginormous proportion.

What dream(s) are you about to birth? It doesn't matter how long you have waited or how challenging the journey, moving day is here and by faith it is done.

Have you heard the term, "Fake it 'til you make it?" Well that's what we're doing. It might not look like it right now, but our change is here: we are business owners, husbands, wives, parents of successful children, philanthropists, award-winning artists, teachers, lawyers, chefs, and pastors. Our marriages thrive, our family members are saved, and we are well—mind, body, and spirit. And this is all possible because we have surrendered our collective wills for God's. Now He is ready to act on our behalf.

Therefore, step out in faith; prepare your provisions, and ACT LIKE YOU ARE ABOUT TO MOVE.

#PTWG

AALIYAH'S AFFIRMATION CORNER: God is going to give me an opportunity I really desire, so I will have faith in Him.

WHAT'S THIS VERSE ABOUT?
Joshua 1:11

_____

_____

_____

KEEPING IT REAL: God isn't going to do everything for you. You have to put in some work too! Are you doing your part?

_____

_____

_____

PRAYER CORNER: Thank you God for reminding me that your promises are yes and amen and that they come to pass. Based on that truth, I am going to act like I'm moving. Let me take my eyes off of what I see and ask for supernatural strength to see what is already done in the Spirit. Because it will be my faith in You that produces the result You have promised. I seal this prayer in the matchless name of Jesus. Amen.

The Promise

All who have given up home or brothers and sisters or
father and mother or children or land for me will be given
a hundred times as much. They will also have eternal life.
(Matthew 19:29)

E xodus 20:2-3 reads, "I am the Lord your God, the one
who brought you out of Egypt where you were slaves.
Do not worship any god except me."

Those words, first spoken to the children of Israel after
their exodus from Egypt, are still relevant today. We are
to put nothing before God because He can and will meet
all of our needs. There is nothing that can replace the love,
joy, and peace that following Him brings. And lest we
forget this truth, He will test us.

Throughout history, God has tested the allegiance of
His people. Abraham was commanded to sacrifice His
son Isaac—the product of his old age and the key to
the fulfillment of God's promises to him. Ruth chose to
stay with Naomi her widowed mother-in-law, rather than
pursue a seemingly better life among her people. Queen
Esther, who had at her disposal all the luxuries that life
could offer, risked her life to save God's people from

destruction. Because of their obedience, their sacrifices were rewarded handsomely; God manifested His glory and blessed them beyond what they would have gained had they acted selfishly. In other words, their sacrifices reaped a hundredfold harvest.

Likewise, we are of this number; we are also the blessed. Some 33 days ago, in a radical act of obedience we responded to God's challenge and surrendered what was dear to us; what we thought sustained our very existence. Collectively, we have sacrificed our idols—food, free-time, cowardice, timidity, unforgiveness, and control—to God, and have pursued Him with all our might.

God has said throughout the course of this fast that our sacrifices have not gone unnoticed. He now promises that He will render a hundredfold blessing; a blessing, in fact, that is exceedingly abundantly above all that we ask or think (see Ephesians 3:20).

It has been a pleasure to be on this journey with you. As we embark upon our last week, let us not neglect to reflect on how far God has brought us. I don't know about you, but I am a different person. The idols of timidity and cowardice have been replaced with courage and boldness, but it is not over yet. I look forward to what God will do for us on next week.

Lastly, God has given us a powerful word this week. To summarize, here's His promise: "I am the God of the impossible; miracles are my specialty and I don't need a lot of time to perform them. If you would allow my grace to empower your every action, I will get the glory, and you will receive all that I have promised, even a hundredfold." Amen.

#PTWG

AALIYAH'S AFFIRMATION CORNER: If I would allow Gods' grace to empower me, He will get the glory, and I will receive all that He has promised, even a hundred times move.

WHAT'S THIS VERSE ABOUT?
Matthew 19:29

_____

_____

_____

KEEPING IT REAL: Do you even want to give your life to God? Or do you want to life like you want to? Explain.

_____

_____

_____

PRAYER CORNER: Dear Heavenly Father, Your kingdom come, Your will be done on earth as it is already done in heaven. Let me release what I think is best, so that I may maintain your best. Let me not be afraid to leave it all for you, for it is only what I do for Christ that will last. In the name of Jesus I pray. Amen.

#PTWG

Scripture(s):

How is God speaking to you today through His Word, through people, or any other way?

#PTWG

Scripture(s):

How is God speaking to you today through His Word, through people, or any other way?

No More Props

The mighty Lord All-Powerful
is going to take away
   from Jerusalem and Judah
everything you need—
   your bread and water,

(Isaiah 3:1)

My Aaliyah, soon to be four years old, has times when she wants to be a baby again, especially when she's feeling frightened. In a futile attempt to regress, she asks for items that represent her babyhood, like a sippy cup or a stroller. When this occurs, AJ, her six-year-old, know-it-all brother, cries out in frustration, "You are not a baby anymore!" In those moments the truth of his declaration is unsettling for her. I can see the agitation on her face as she attempts to embrace her new reality: *I am a big girl now.*

This truth, *I am a big girl/boy now,* can also be unsettling for the believer. As babes in Christ, He gives us all sorts of baby items or "props" that enable us to succeed. These props can include new member's classes, extensive guidance from godly mentors, and affiliation with certain beginner-type ministries, yet there comes a time when we have to grow up. It is then that He removes every prop and requires us to stand on our own. This season can be scary, but the Holy Spirit, our comforter, is right there to guide and gently remind us that we are no longer babes in Christ.

By way of this prop-removing process, I have gone from a babe in the faith to a budding powerhouse. At the top of this year, God required that I drop most of every activity that brought me a sense of fulfillment. He isolated me and begun the process of my knowing Him for myself. The first thing that He did was reveal to me a startling truth: I had grown far too reliant on other people's faith. I had become accustomed to depending on others to tell me what God was saying, but now that needed to be my responsibility.

For example, my parents, pillars of faith, had been one of my props. Whenever a crisis arose I would run straight to them. When I was diagnosed with cancer, my mother's prophesy "this is not until death" fueled my faith. When my friend suffered a stroke, my dad's words, "she will fully recover," fueled our faith. But now God is saying *No More*. He has removed every prop and now I have to hear God for myself and speak just as He instructs. I must admit it's kind of frightening, yet necessary for my growth.

Amazingly, I woke up this morning humming the song "Jesus is Real," by Pastor John P. Kee. The lyrics, "Jesus is real, I know the Lord is real to me," played over and over in my head. That is now AALIYAH SPEAKS. My prayer partner had prophesied some months back that this was the season for us to "see God." I didn't understand then, but now I do. God has removed every prop so that I can see and know Him for myself.

Perhaps you are experiencing something similar and God has removed all your props. If so, you will no longer be able to depend on your parents, pastor, TV evangelist, ministry leaders and mentors for a word. He is requiring you know His voice for yourself.

Paul wrote, "When we were children, we thought and reasoned as children do. But when we grew up, we quit our childish ways." (I Corinthians 13:11).

Depending solely on other people to hear a word from God is childish. It is time that we hear, believe, and speak God's truth as He has spoken it to us. We need to not be afraid; we need to not regress to our babyhood in Christ. The props have been removed and in their place lay supernatural faith that will turn this world upside down.

#PTWG

---○---

AALIYAH'S AFFIRMATION CORNER: Depending solely on other people to hear a word from God is childish. It is time that I hear, believe, and speak God's truth as He has spoken it to me. Even as a teen!

WHAT'S THIS VERSE ABOUT?
Isaiah 3:1

_____

_____

_____

KEEPING IT REAL: Have you made sacrifices in the past? Did God reward you?

_____

_____

_____

PRAYER CORNER: God thank you for speaking to me. I'm grateful that I know your voice. Help me to be brave. Encourage me as only you can to step out into the deep. There is nothing to fear and so much to be gained. In Jesus' Name I pray. Amen.

Reject Rejection

My followers, whoever listens to you is listening to me.
Anyone who says "No" to you is saying "No" to me.
And anyone who says "No" to me is really saying "No"
to the one who sent me.

(Luke 10:16)

During His public ministry, Jesus chose and appointed seventy men to go two by two into every town and place, where He Himself would eventually enter, to minister the good news of the gospel (see Luke 10:1). He urged them to be productive and to operate according to the authority given to them.

The seventy did as instructed. With passion they preached "the kingdom of God is at hand," with authority they cast out demons, and without provocation they spoke blessings over those who received them and warnings to those who did not. Even in the face of outright rejection they wouldn't fear or change the message; they simply kicked the dust off their feet and moved on.

My father accepted Christ when I was six years old. He and his radical Christian friends were on-fire for God, and didn't mind letting the world know. In their zeal—and to my horror—they started a street ministry. My friends would ask, "Didn't I see your father preaching on the corner?" I would quickly deny I knew such a man. But yes, it was my father and his friends preaching on the streets.

Despite the rejection, which was great, they were fearless. Passersby would cross to the other side, roll their eyes, plug their ears and verbally fight their message, yet they weren't deterred. They understood, as we should today, that the rejection was not about them, but Christ. Through it all they learned to reject rejection.

Rejecting rejection is not innate. Everything in us screams that we should avoid rejection at all costs, but today we are being instructed to reject rejection.

You may not have a street ministry like my dad or find yourself going from place to place like the seventy, but you do have an obligation to preach the good news of the gospel to those around you, by word and deed. Don't fret if family, friends, and/or co-workers are less than thrilled with the "new" you who has emerged as a result of this fast. My friend, that just comes with the territory. No matter what, simply tell them the truth of God's word and if they reject it, shake the dust off your feet and keep moving.

I truly hope you realize that you are different as a result of this fast; no one can have an encounter with God and remain unchanged. Therefore, be about your father's business and do what He requires. He will use you to call into existence that which is not, to move mountains in faith, and to draw men to Him. Over time, you will have the same testimony as the seventy, who reported to Jesus, "Lord, even the demons are subject to us in Your name." Praise God that we have all authority over the enemy so there is nothing to fear. Therefore, keep the faith, do as instructed, and learn to reject rejection.

#PTWG

AALIYAH'S AFFIRMATION CORNER: I will have radical faith and because of my faith God will use me to call speak into existence things that don't exist yet.

WHAT'S THIS VERSE ABOUT?
Luke 10:16

_____

_____

_____

KEEPING IT REAL: How do you feel when people reject you? Do you think there are times that God rejects you?

_____

_____

_____

PRAYER CORNER: God thank you for the reminder that I am to reject rejection. It's not easy, but I know in you all things are possible. Lord help me to be confident in what you have called me to do. Let me not be swayed by my own lust, but to be spiritually-minded so that I can pursue what is of You. Your plan is best and I say yes to it today and forever. In Jesus' Name I pray. Amen.

Childlike Humility

But if you are as humble as this child, you are the
greatest in the kingdom of heaven.
(Matthew 18:4)

It occurred to me this morning that God is ministering
His final instructions to us. Monday: *No More Props*;
yesterday: *Reject Rejection*, and today: *Childlike Humility*.
For that reason, "If you have ears, listen to what the Spirit
says to the churches" (Revelations 2:17).

At the top of Matthew 18, Jesus' disciples came to
Him and asked, "Who then is greatest in the kingdom of
heaven?" Jesus, in typical fashion, delivered His answer
through demonstration. He called to Himself a child and
said, "I promise you this. If you don't change and become
like a child, you will never get into the kingdom of heaven."
(Matthew 18:3).

As believers we know that we are destined for heaven,
but the kingdom that Jesus speaks of in Matthew 18 is
God's kingdom here on earth. Each of us has been
bestowed a kingdom often called "destiny" which is our
place of assignment. Our arrival to this place is determined
by God, but also contingent on our mindset. Without the

proper mindset we will never arrive. Take the children of Israel for example. Their complaining and arrogance robbed them of the opportunity to inhabit the land flowing with milk and honey.

The destiny mindset is one of total surrender and complete humility. The word humility is derived from the word humble which means not proud or haughty. When one is humble, he lives a life of submission and considers himself low in a hierarchy. He isn't vying for position, stepping on others to advance, and merely concentrating on his own needs. No, the humble believer is like a child.

Children are amazing to watch. I have the pleasure of parenting two wonderful little gifts. Unfortunately, there are times when they behave improperly and must be chastised. Even then...one minute they are crying and angry, but the next lowly and apologetic, as they hug me about the legs.

That is what our heavenly father requires of us: a complete surrender and trust of His plan. He isn't looking for the smartest and the brightest, or requiring us to have degrees and other achievements, for surely "the last will be first, and the first last." He simply seeks whom He can use for the edifying and building of His kingdom.

This fast has been about exercising a spirit of humility; about ridding ourselves of the hindrances that keep us from being all God requires. It hasn't been easy but well worth the effort. Ironically enough, we started this fast with a discussion on humility (see *Expect the Unexpected*) and ended with the same. It is clear that we need humility to be all that God has called us to be.

Lastly, I thank God for His purging process. We are now better equipped for kingdom work because we have exercised, through surrender, childlike humility.

#PTWG

AALIYAH'S AFFIRMATION CORNER: As a teen I will do whatever it takes to please God.

WHAT'S THIS VERSE ABOUT?
Matthew 18:4

_____

_____

_____

KEEPING IT REAL: Why do you think humility is important to God?

_____

_____

_____

PRAYER CORNER: Lord thank you for this word today. Thank you for the call that is on my life. Greatness is on me and all you ask is that I position myself to be humble. I surrender pride today and take on the garment of humility instead. Just as you have said in your word when I humble myself before you, you will lift me up. Thank you for that promise. In Jesus' Name I pray. Amen.

Wait on the Lord

I, the Lord your God, will make up for the losses
caused by those swarms and swarms of locusts I sent
to attack you.
My people, you will eat until you are satisfied.
Then you will praise me for the wonderful things
I have done.
Never again will you be put to shame.
(Joel 2:25-26)

At 61, my dad is in the prime of His life. He is the husband
of Malinda, his bride of 41 years, the father to 8 saved
children, grandfather to 12, the Pastor of 2 churches, the
Superintendent/Overseer for 4 other churches, the owner
of a lovely home and two luxury vehicles.

It hasn't always been that way; growing up, finances were
tight. My dad, the sole bread-winner, was often in and out
of work. All ten of us shared a three bedroom home with
one bath. The church van was often our primary mode of
transport. We always had dinner, but I know there were
times when my parents weren't sure how the Lord would
provide. We used food stamps, ate government cheese,
and wore hand-me-downs (well, at least my siblings did,

one of the perks of being the oldest was that I was able to wear each item first!)

Regardless of the challenges he faced, my dad never allowed the circumstances to deter him from his proper position in the home; he always gave his family his best. All the while, God was watching and storing up his blessings.

At the same time, my dad was an associate minister with a local congregation. He sat under that leadership for many years. While others would've been itching to get their own church, my dad was unwilling to move without God's leading. All the while, God was watching and storing up his blessings.

My dad was in poor health in his 40s. At 42, his mother died of a massive heart attack. Accordingly, he had his first heart attack at 42 and a few years later another. Yet again, he remained faithful. All the while, God was watching and storing up his blessings.

Needless to say, the locust had eaten a lot, and things didn't look good—but God; He is never slack concerning His promises. Over those years, God had spoken many wonderful blessings over my dad's life—that he would have a beautiful home, he would place in him a new (physical) heart, and that he would pastor many. Because His word will not return to Him void, those promises had to come to pass. Although my dad's circumstances often looked bleak, he chose to believe God. Now his faith is being rewarded and he is enjoying the fruit of his labor and basking in

God's overflow. As promised, God has restored all the years the locust had eaten and my dad is not ashamed.

Maybe you can only relate to the first portion of my dad's story. Maybe you're struggling, unsure of God's plan, and growing weary with each passing day. Well don't give up. God is watching and storing up your blessings.

Today, my dad and mom are shining examples of what waiting on the Lord looks like. Because God is faithful; He has restored them completely and they are being drenched in His latter rain. In fact, He is preparing them for even more, including international ministry. Who says God can't make up for (what we perceive as) lost time? He can and will restore!

As God has said repeatedly during the course of this fast, your surrender has not gone unnoticed. Your willingness to submit to His plan for these last 39 days has caused Him to store blessings on your behalf. You may be seeing some of the benefits now, but that's only the beginning. You have an abundant harvest waiting on you, so don't give up.

Wait on the Lord and be of good courage. You will bask in the overflow and reap an abundant harvest if you faint not. No matter what the locust has eaten or stolen, God will restore it ALL and you will not be put to shame. Amen.

#PTWG

AALIYAH'S AFFIRMATION CORNER: I am going to wait on the Lord and not complain.

WHAT'S THIS VERSE ABOUT?
Joel 2:26-26

_____
_____
_____

KEEPING IT REAL: During this fast, how has God made changes in your life?

_____
_____
_____

PRAYER CORNER: Thank you Lord for your promise to restore all that was taken from me. I will patiently wait on you. I will continue to be consistent and faithful in what you have called me to do, knowing that your plan is best. And I know that I will never be put to shame. In Jesus' Name I pray. Amen.

God Has Done a New Thing

Welcome to Day 40! What a journey this has been. You may recall that we started this journey with these words: *Let God Do a New Thing* and thus appropriately ending with this phrase: *God Has Done a New Thing*.

God told us from the beginning to simply give Him 40 days and a surrendered heart and He would change our lives. I praise Him for what He has done! The song, *Marvelous* by the late Bishop Walter Hawkins is ringing in my spirit:

> *I will sing your praise*
> *for you've done such a Marvelous thing.*
> *For someone so wretched*
> *yet my soul you have redeemed*
>
> *No one else could do it.*
> *No one could care half as much.*
> *Yet you thought my soul was worth it.*
> *So you gave your only son.*
>
> *You gave that I might live.*
> *You gave that I might be set free.*
> *Exchanged your life for mine.*
> *What a Marvelous thing you've done.*

I am appropriately silenced this morning. I simply hear God saying, "Praise the Lord and pray in his name!" (Psalm 105:1a)! Take the time this morning and throughout the weekend to reflect on what God has done during these 40-days. I pray that you have allowed Him to do a new thing in you. Be blessed!

#PTWG

AALIYAH'S AFFIRMATION CORNER: God can be trusted. I surrender all.

WHAT'S THIS VERSE ABOUT?
Psalm 105:1a

_____
_____
_____

KEEPING IT REAL: Were you blessed by being on this fast? Name the best thing that has happened.

_____
_____
_____

PRAYER CORNER: Thank you God for bringing me through 40 days of fasting. My life will never be the same. I will engage the world differently because of this time that I have spent with you. God pour out on me as never before. Continue to keep me well spirit, mind, and body. Lord thank you for the favor you have given me in my home, on my job and with everyone that I encounter. Thank you for new life, renewed purpose and the determination to complete the assignment for which you have brought me to earth to do. In Jesus' Name I pray. Amen.

ABOUT THE AUTHORS

Dr. Celeste Owens is a sought-after speaker and facilitator whose mission is to equip people to live free and whole through surrender of mind, body, and spirit. A transformative healer, she uses the word of God and psychological principles to bring others to total wellness.

Dr. Celeste and her husband, Andel co-founded Dr. Celeste Owens Ministries, an international healing ministry and travel the globe sharing the philosophy of surrender. They believe that when God is the center there is nothing one can't do!

Surrender is what Dr. Celeste does. She will continue to encourage others where ever she may go to do God's Will—His Way—All the Time!

Aaliyah Owens is a teen living with her mom Dr. Celeste, dad Andel and brother AJ (the author of The 40-Day Surrender fast for Kids). She wants to be a surgeon when she grows up. She also loves dance especially ballet and learning about new people and cultures. She especially has a heart for people and has a strong interest in social justice.

Learn more at drcelesteowens.com

www.ingramcontent.com/pod-product-compliance
Lightning Source LLC
LaVergne TN
LVHW051122080426
835510LV00018B/2187

9 781735 588209